T0322425

BRITISH LEYLAND

MOTOR CORPORATION

1968-2005
THE STORY FROM INSIDE

MIKE CARVER, NICK SEALE, ANNE YOUNGSON

The History Press

Cover illustrations: Front: Work on the Austin Montego. (HMC); *Back:* The Rover 3500, launched in 1976. (HMC)

Foreword and chapter 13 illustrations © Jaguar Land Rover.

Chapters 1–11 illustrations are from publicity material (including brochures and photographs) originally produced by the British Leyland Motor Corporation (subsequently British Leyland Ltd and later Rover Group Ltd) and its constituent companies including Austin, Vanden Plas, Morris, MG, Riley, Wolseley, the Nuffield Organisation, the British Motor Corporation, British Motor Holdings, Rover, Standard, Triumph, and the Leyland Motor Corporation. Material is the copyright of the British Motor Industry Heritage Trust and is reproduced in this publication with their permission.

First published 2015

The History Press
The Mill, Brimscombe Port
Stroud, Gloucestershire, GL5 2QG
www.thehistorypress.co.uk

Reprinted 2015

© Mike Carver, Nick Seale, Anne Youngson, 2015

The right of Mike Carver, Nick Seale, Anne Youngson to be identified as the Authors of this work has been asserted in accordance with the Copyright, Designs and Patents Act 1988.

British Library Cataloguing in Publication Data.
A catalogue record for this book is available from the British Library.

ISBN 978 0 7509 6144 8

Typesetting and origination by The History Press
Printed in Great Britain by TJ International Ltd, Padstow, Cornwall

Contents

Foreword

The British Leyland Motor Corporation (BLMC) was created in 1968 by bringing together almost all the British-owned car and commercial vehicle companies that then existed. The resulting conglomerate formed the sixth largest car manufacturer in the world motor industry, confidently expected to give the United Kingdom a leading and enduring place in that industry. In April 2005 the tiny remains of the group went into administration, bringing to an ignominious end a venture of which so much had been expected and on which so much effort and so much national resource had been expended.

Nevertheless, although the failure was one of the biggest and most disappointing disasters in British industrial history, there were a limited number of successes, one of which, the reform of industrial relations led by Sir Michael Edwardes, was not only important for the motor industry but was the launch pad for the wholesale national reform of industrial relations in the United Kingdom. An understanding of the reasons for the failures and the successes is still important for the future of British industry. Up to now there is little consensus on this in spite of much debate and writing, mainly by academics and journalists.

This book is written by three people who worked for BLMC in various roles and at various levels through most of the period of decline and who were involved in much of what happened. They are therefore able to bring an unusual degree of insight to the analysis of what happened and why.

In writing this book, the authors have concentrated on cars. The group at its formation was a conglomerate of many sorts of vehicle companies, but by far the largest component, on which success or failure of the whole group depended, was that embracing the cars businesses. However, it is not possible to divorce completely the events affecting cars from the rest – for instance, there are no authoritative financial figures for cars alone. However, most of the events, decisions and outcomes that did affect cars were separate from those affecting the rest of the group, and enable the story of cars to be isolated from the rest clearly and accurately.

Well before the formation of BLMC it had been the widely-held view that the British car industry was too fragmented to succeed and needed consolidating. Thus the origins of BLMC and its inherited strengths and its weaknesses lie in the years before its actual formation. The book therefore starts with a brief account of the industry in those years, followed by a narrative of events until the end came and an analysis of the reasons for the failure.

Finally, as an epilogue, we provide a brief summary of the relatively healthy state that the UK motor industry is in today. In particular we describe the success of the brands Jaguar, Land Rover, Range Rover, Mini and MG that have survived the demise of BLMC.ß

The success of the Range Rover Evoque characterises the resurgence of BLMC's legacy brands.

Prologue

Formation of the British Leyland Motor Corporation

From the early years of the car, British car manufacturing was strong, and by 1938 it was clearly in second place among car-producing countries. In 1938 the country produced 341,000 vehicles, a long way behind the USA, which produced 2 million in that year, but ahead of Germany which produced 277,000.

After the Second World War, the factories that had been channelled into the war effort were converted back to car manufacture and by 1950 new models were being introduced and production was 53 per cent higher than in 1938. Underlying this growth there were structural problems, which had been recognised by the UK government as early as 1945. The Political and Economic Planning Group formed the view that there were too many companies producing at 'uneconomically low annual volumes'. The industry needed rationalisation and part standardisation to achieve economies of scale. But by 1950 very little had changed. World car catalogues of the day showed that there were thirty-three distinct British car brands. This was more than the entire offering of the whole of continental Europe.

While the UK car industry had recovered from the war, the same was not true of the rest of Europe where in 1950 volumes had only just reached pre-war levels. A real boom, however, had taken place in the USA. Production had trebled to 6 million and this boom was to give the big three US manufacturers, GM, Ford and Chrysler, the resources to invest heavily in Europe where the 1950s was a period of great change.

Encouraged by the government, the UK's two largest companies, Austin and the Nuffield Group, merged in 1952, bringing together the Austin, Morris, Wolseley, Riley, Austin-Healey and MG brands to form the British Motor Corporation (BMC). This new company held more than 50 per cent of the UK market and was substantially larger than any other European car company.

The Mini was launched in 1959 and the last Mini, shown here, was produced on 4 October 2000.

Elsewhere the Rootes Group brought together the Hillman, Humber, Singer and Sunbeam brands, while Standard and Triumph were integrating their activities, having merged in 1938. A few smaller manufacturers like Jowett, Lea Francis, Frazer Nash and Armstrong Siddeley went out of business.

By the mid 1950s over 90 per cent of the UK industry was made up of five companies – BMC, Ford, the Rootes Group, Vauxhall (GM since 1925) and Standard Triumph.

In Europe the picture was different. Companies were expanding on the back of rapid market growth. Between 1950 and 1960 there was a fivefold increase in production volumes. The fastest-growing company was VW, which had increased from 97,000 in 1950 to 787,000 in 1960. This growth was based solely on the enormous success of the Beetle, the only model that VW produced at that time. Although the Beetle was fundamentally a pre-war design, its sales were based on an unrivalled reputation for reliability and durability. This gave VW a presence in virtually every car market in the world. Opel and Ford in Germany also experienced rapid expansion in the 1950s, benefitting from heavy investment from their American parent companies.

Issigonis started working on a new Mini in 1967 (9X). The project was shelved by BLMC.

European growth was achieved without model proliferation. No high-volume manufacturer produced more than four models, whereas BMC continued with a range of ten or eleven models throughout the '50s. It was proving difficult for BMC to achieve economies of scale while maintaining the separate brands, sales networks and factories that it had inherited in the merger. It is also unclear whether rationalisation was pursued vigorously by the senior management or indeed whether the need for it was even recognised as a priority.

By the end of the 1950s, BMC had fallen behind VW but was still the second largest car manufacturer in Europe. However, it was just about to launch two groundbreaking products, the Mini in 1959 and the Morris/Austin 1100 in 1962. Both models were far superior in terms of space utilisation and roadholding to any other car in their sectors – the highest volume sectors of the European car market. Pinin Farina had produced an attractive design for the 1100 and it was an immediate sales success. From 1964 to 1971 it was the UK's highest-selling car, achieving 15 per cent of the market at its peak. The Mini took longer to reach market acceptability, but by 1965 it was firmly in third place in the UK market with a share of 10 per cent. (The Ford Cortina was in second place with a share of 12 per cent.)

Additionally, BMC owned the well-respected MG and Austin-Healey sports car brands. The small MG Midget and MGA (replaced in 1962 by the MGB) were particularly successful in the US market .

With these models, the 1960s should therefore have been a period of prosperity for BMC. This was far from the reality. By the end of 1967, BMC's UK market share had fallen from 50 per cent to 30 per cent, total annual volumes were 11 per cent lower than in 1960 and the company was losing money.

While BMC was struggling, European manufacturers were growing strongly throughout the 1960s, increasing production by 50 per cent. VW was now making more than a million vehicles a year, having added a bigger saloon to its product range, and was exporting over 60 per cent, with the US as its major market.

One significant factor was that economic growth within the European Economic Community (EEC, forerunner of the EU) averaged 4–5 per cent annual GDP growth and was very much higher than the 2–3 per cent achieved within the European Free Trade Association (EFTA, of which the UK was a member). From 1960 to 1967, the car market grew by 92 per cent within the EEC compared with 39 per cent in the UK.

In the UK, Ford was putting pressure on BMC. Ford's new product and facility investment was running at over 10 per cent of revenue, whereas BMC was investing at less than 5 per cent of revenue. In the mid 1960s Ford UK made virtually no profit. The parent was adopting an aggressive strategy to win market share and its target was BMC. By 1967, Ford's market share was only four percentage points behind BMC. The Cortina was its most successful product; BMC could not match its 1500/1600cc engine size and had no modern attractive product to compete in the mid sector of the market.

BMC's initial response was to launch the Austin 1800 in 1964. However, the concept was ill judged. Adherence to the front-wheel-drive layout, so successful in the Mini and the 1100, created a car that was too wide and too high to be a true competitor to the Cortina. The resulting ungainly vehicle justifiably became known as the 'Land Crab', and understandably sales fell well short of projections.

Rather than address the problem of the mid sector immediately, BMC decided to put its new product resources into developing the executive Austin 3 Litre, which was launched in 1967. If the Austin 1800 concept was ill-judged, the 3 Litre was disastrous. Austin had never been successful in the executive sector. The 3 Litre's suspension was an engineering tour

The outstandingly succesful Jaguar XJS was under development before the merger and was the first model launched by BLMC in 1968.

de force, but the car was underpowered and badly proportioned. Perhaps worst of all, the in-house styling was dictated by the use of Austin 1800 doors. These were available because the new door-manufacturing line was severely underutilised. (This fatal mistake was repeated in the desperately needed Austin Maxi, BMC's gift to the newly formed BLMC in 1969.) Inevitably, sales of the 3 Litre were very low.

BMC was also finding it hard to rationalise its models and components. Despite the undoubted success of the 1100, BMC was unwilling to stop producing the models that needed replacement. Both the Austin A40 and the Morris Minor continued in production for at least five years after the 1100 launch.

Misguided product planning was not the only reason for BMC's poor performance in the 1960s; its cost management was weak. Product costs were high because of expensive product design, inefficient manufacturing processes, low labour productivity, component complexity and poor economies of scale. Several models had marginal profitability. In particular, a well-publicised study by Ford had demonstrated that the Mini, which had become BMC's highest seller in most European markets, was being sold at a loss.

Labour relations were notoriously bad. Strikes occurred throughout UK manufacturing, but the car industry was one of the worst affected. Soon after the creation of BLMC, the Employment Minister, Barbara Castle, tried to start a new relationship between unions and employers with the publication of a White Paper entitled 'In Place of Strife'. However, she found it impossible to reach a consensus and the status quo remained. Poor labour relations were to remain a continuing issue for BLMC. The UK was not alone in suffering disputes between employees and employers, but by the late 1960s companies like VW and Toyota had achieved a much more cooperative relationship. At VW, for example, a workers' representative had a place on the board.

Britain's exclusion from the EEC had an impact on BMC. Import tariffs caused the company to set up an assembly plant in 1965 at Seneffe in Belgium, diverting financial and management resources away from the core business. BMC also licensed Innocenti in Italy to manufacture the Mini, a successful arrangement producing up to 50,000 vehicles a year.

Most critically of all, BMC was losing its reputation for quality and reliability. The reasons for this failure were numerous. VW had demonstrated the value of achieving high standards and the resulting positive reputation. For some reason the senior management seemed to lose sight of the need to satisfy customers and did not make this a priority throughout the company. It was all too easy to accept the paradigm 'high price = high quality, low price = low quality'. Throughout the company, responsibility for problem resolution was unclear. Engineers, manufacturing management and suppliers would prefer to blame each other rather than protect the customer. In the US the quality of British cars' electrical systems was regarded as so poor that the supplier, Lucas, became known as 'Prince of Darkness'.

As BMC faltered, Leyland Motors thrived. Since the Second World War, Leyland had been growing through acquisition. Its core business was in commercial vehicles; it had purchased Albion in 1951, Scammell in 1955, AEC, Thorneycroft, Park Royal and Charles Roe in 1962, Bristol Commercial Vehicles in 1965 and finally Aveling Barford in 1967.

In 1960, Leyland took over Standard Triumph. The Standard brand was dropped and Triumph undertook an ambitious product programme, introducing the TR4 sports car in 1961, the Vitesse, a small sporting saloon in 1962, the 2000, a larger sporting saloon in 1963 and the 1300, a small premium front-wheel-drive saloon, in 1965. Triumph's volumes were small in comparison to BMC (122,000 vs 537,000 in 1967) but had grown throughout the 1960s and its UK market share in 1967 was 8.5 per cent. Like BMC, Triumph opened a small assembly plant at Malines in Belgium in 1962. Significantly, Triumph had succeeded in gaining a reputation for product quality, which allowed it to justify premium pricing.

In 1967 Leyland took over Rover. Rover was a historically staid company producing luxury saloons and the utility Land Rover. In 1963 it broke the mould when it launched, to great acclaim, the Rover 2000. This model competed directly with the Triumph 2000, marginally outselling it. Although Rover was now producing more saloon cars than at any time in its history, the utility Land Rover was its highest volume and most profitable product with an annual volume of 36,000.

In 1966 Jaguar, fearing that it did not have the financial strength to fund its new models, had joined BMC. All major British-owned brands were therefore owned by Leyland and BMC. The government then encouraged Leyland and BMC to merge, convinced that scale was essential for long-term survival. However, at that time BMC's assets and share value were greater than Leyland's. Donald Stokes, managing director of Leyland, declined the proposal because he was unwilling to be a junior partner in any merger. Eighteen months later the situation was different. BMC's poor results had reduced its share price. Leyland's acquisition of Rover and Aveling Barford had increased its asset value and share price. The merger could now take place with Leyland, with Stokes at the helm. On 17 January 1968 the formation of the British Leyland Motor Corporation (BLMC) was announced.

Pundits were optimistic about the future. BLMC was the sixth largest motor manufacturer in the world after GM, Ford, Chrysler, Fiat and VW. It held 41 per cent of the UK car market with the first and third bestselling vehicles. With MG, Triumph and Jaguar, it held a dominant position in the sports car market, which was thriving in the US. The Land Rover had established its own niche. Rover and Triumph were now accepted as premium brands and together were twice the size of the growing BMW. The commercial vehicles under the Leyland umbrella were market leaders in virtually every sector.

Nevertheless, as already stated, there were many weaknesses in the car companies on which the success of the venture depended, and bringing those companies together would require a great deal of foresight while at the same time repairing the many weaknesses.

Critically, the car line-up bore no comparison with any of its competitors:

	BLMC	VW	Ford	Renault	Citroen	Opel	Daimler-Benz
Brands	11	1	1	1	1	1	1
Model Lines	21	3	5	4	3	3	5
Volumes '000s pa	762	1089	441	707	419	540	200

The difference was essentially due to BLMC consisting of four car-producing companies before any rationalisation, between them serving three different market sectors (volume cars, specialist cars and sports cars) compared with the other listed companies, which all produced cars, with a very few minor exceptions, for the volume car market. This made rationalisation even more complicated than the bare figures in the above table indicate.

Overall control of the whole corporation was to be exercised by an eleven-man board composed of eight executive directors and three non-executive directors.:

Chairman and Managing Director	Sir Donald (later Lord) Stokes
Deputy Chairman and Chairman/ Chief Executive of Jaguar	Sir William Lyons
Deputy Chairman –Non-executive	L.G. Whyte
Deputy MD and Director of Engineering	Dr A. Fogg
Deputy MD with special responsibilities for Overseas Operations	J.H. Plane
Deputy MD and MD Austin-Morris	G.H. Turnbull
Director of Finance and Planning	J.N.R. Barber
Director, Austin-Morris	R.J. Lucas
Chairman of Rover	Sir George Farmer
Non-executives	R.A. Stormonth-Darling and J.D. Slater

Before the formation of BLMC, Lord Stokes had been deputy chairman and managing director of the Leyland Motor Corporation; Sir William Lyons chairman of Jaguar, Sir George Farmer chairman of Rover; G.H. Turnbull managing director of the Triumph Car Company; Dr Fogg director of engineering for Leyland Trucks; R.J. Lucas company secretary of BMH; J.H. Plane was a South African businessman with extensive business interests there; J.N.R. Barber had been finance director of Ford of Britain and more recently finance director of AEC; R.A. Stormonth-Darling and J.D.Slater were prominent businessmen.

The group that the board had to control consisted of a headquarters and the following operating divisions:

Austin-Morris Division
Specialist Car Division
Truck and Bus Division
Foundry and General Engineering Division
Pressed Steel Fisher Division
Construction Equipment Division
Overseas Division

The headquarters was established in Berkeley Square in London and the new company came into being officially on 17 January 1968.

1

High Expectations
Confounded: 1968–75

Those responsible (the government through the Industrial Reorganisation Corporation, and the companies themselves, apprehensive about remaining alone and too small to survive) for putting the new corporation together saw certain opportunities in BLMC: its size would provide the means for successful growth and the ability to concentrate resources by rationalisation would save money and raise the standard of each new product. This last belief in particular was strongly held by many of the management, who clearly assumed that the performance standards of the concentrated activities were, or could be made to be, of a sort and standard to compete with the rest of the world. Thus the formation of BLMC was seen as the opportunity for building a company that would be a powerful force in the world motor industry.

It will help to understand what happened in the early years if those beliefs and assumptions are examined to see how realistic they were.

The first matter to consider is whether it was realistic to expect to draw into a coherent whole the many and varied companies that were being brought together. The companies involved were designing and producing a range of cars that covered just about the whole car market, the same for commercial vehicles and then a wide variety of such things as construction vehicles and equipment, rounded off by the production of refrigeration equipment and a printing works.

The British Motor Holdings 1967 company report included the following list:

- Austin, Austin-Healey, MG, Morris, Vanden Plas Princess R, Wolseley and Riley cars, Austin and Morris Mini-Cooper cars.
- Austin and Morris light vans, light commercial vehicles, trucks, tractors and Gipsy cross-country vehicles
- Jaguar and Daimler cars
- Daimler buses and military vehicles
- Guy trucks and buses
- Vehicle bodies and press tools for the motor industry
- Marine and industrial engines
- SU Carburettors
- Fisholow and Gridway products and domestic appliances
- Prestcold refrigeration equipment
- Nuffield Press

In fact, on closer examination things were not quite as difficult as they looked. The companies fell into three groups – Cars, Commercial Vehicles and a miscellaneous group broadly related to construction. These three groups were operationally and commercially very different from one another and required little rationalisation with one another. However, as part of BLMC they would need to adopt common administrative practices in such things as financial reporting, controls over investment and matters of major policy. Within each group, and BLMC-wide in some cases, there would have to be common terms of employment, payment structures and so on. Changing all these practices would take a lot of planning, explanation, discussion and administrative effort before they could be put into practice. This would take time, but there would be no great practical difficulties in the way – except the not-to-be-underestimated inbuilt resistance to any changes to the existing company cultures, different for each company and ingrained over many years.

The greater problem is the much more important matter of rationalising a company's product range and with that its production facilities and design and development resources and practices. This rationalisation can apply both within one company and, with more difficulty, between companies. Within BLMC this work lay almost entirely in the Cars Group, by far the biggest of the groups and on whose success the whole future of BLMC depended. The other groups had much less need for product rationalisation within their companies, little between companies and almost none with the other groups.

In the Cars Group, rationalisation was needed both within companies and between companies. On paper, a logical and coordinated range of models and major components could be planned with relative ease. In practice, to replace an established wide model range with a more limited one to be produced in the same, or perhaps greater, volume than the wider range being replaced has many difficulties. New models cannot be developed and brought into production quickly, even if unlimited resources are available – and BLMC resources were limited not only in numbers but also in skill. Introducing several new models in a relatively short time requires more investment in a given period than that needed for a properly spaced and steady replacement cycle. Over and above this, if a new model is to replace more than one existing model there may not be enough appropriate production capacity available to produce the higher volumes of the new model, especially if the replaced models were produced in more than one factory, and so yet more extra investment is required.

The same thing was true for engines. When BLMC was formed it was producing eleven unrelated engines between 1 and 4 litres. Of these, only BMC's 15-year-old A series was made at a competitive scale. The investment required at that time for new high-volume engines involved large transfer lines. The investment cost per unit of capacity was broadly similar for engines and vehicles. New vehicles were expected to generate additional sales, but it was hard to see that investment in engines would have the same result. In an investment-constrained environment, vehicle investment was to take priority.

Whether the vehicle range or the engine line-up is rationalised, the factories not needed must be closed. With the trade unions' attitude to plant closure, BLMC faced a very formidable task indeed in the early years.

The rationalising of the model range also brings other risks. The first is that the normal level of production will not be maintained while the changes are being made. The second is that a reduction in the model range will bring a loss of sales even if the new models are of a higher standard than the old ones, because the limited range will entail the dropping of some marques. Buyers, however illogically, may have a loyalty to one of the dropped marques and will not necessarily turn to its supposed replacement under a different marque name.

To add to these difficulties, the very senior management in the companies were mainly hostile to the centralisation and rationalisation. Given that the constituent companies had been independent (this was true even of Austin and Morris, even though they had together formed BMC for some years), it was inevitable that most of the executive board members who had their own operating empires would be strongly in favour of being allowed to continue without interference from the centre. In this view they were supported by almost all their company management and workforce

Thus there were many risks facing the most important part of BLMC – the cars business. However, within the Cars Group there were strengths. One was that Austin-Morris had a core range of successful high-volume front-wheel-drive cars (Mini, 1100/1300) that was ahead of its time. Subsequently all the successful European manufacturers based their product line-ups on such a range of front-wheel-drive models, but at the time of BLMC's formation Austin-Morris was leading the world. This leadership, properly developed, gave it a great chance to prosper. Other product strengths lay in the Jaguar and Rover brand and, most of all (although not well perceived in BLMC), in Land Rover.

One of the biggest risks (perhaps the biggest) lay in the very poor state of industrial relations. There were many, many bargaining units – each product company had several. Any serious change to working practices had to be taken to the unions and they normally opposed any change, so everything had to be argued about, which took a long time, and the bosses of the companies – the Managing Directors and Manufacturing management – spent their time dealing with the unions and were not able to concentrate on manufacturing improvements. In the end, they came to ignore the task of making improvements.

Inevitably, strikes were frequent, directly costing sales and steadily eroding customer confidence – and indeed becoming something of a public joke. They also had serious practical effects – in Austin-Morris, when production facilities were installed they were made larger than forecast demand indicated to allow for production losses from strikes. Between this and the inability to improve manufacturing efficiency, it was clear a great improvement in industrial relations had to be made if BLMC was to be successful. Bringing about this improvement would require great management determination and skill.

One other big risk was that the product development resources, especially the skills, in the Cars Group, particularly Austin-Morris, would not be adequate for the task of producing the more limited range of new 'better' models. Both the Mini and the 1100/1300 ranges had been just about competitive in quality and reliability for their time on introduction, but there were ominous signs of falling behind, referred to in the Prologue. The Maxi, which was in development at the time of the merger and which was launched in 1969, was to fall well below competitive standards despite its good innovative concept. The risk that new models would be anything but completely competitive was as serious as that posed by poor industrial relations.

The third serious risk came from profitability levels. The 1968 after-tax profit of £20 million on sales of £974 million was quite inadequate. As already said, the hope of those responsible for the formation of BLMC seems to have been that rationalisation would raise profitability to adequate levels. Even this (defining rationalisation as making BLMC into one coherent whole) was unlikely to be enough. Improvements in matters that would not come directly from rationalisation, such as industrial relations and standards of operational performance, particularly in product development and manufacturing in cars, would certainly be needed as well.

Altogether, turning BLMC into a successful, sustainable company was going to be a tough mission – not just because of the task of rationalisation, but because there were serious risks to the rationalised company from the poor state of industrial relations, doubts about product development strength and an underlying financial weakness.

The seriousness of these risks seems not to have been fully foreseen by those responsible for putting BLMC together, or it was believed to be outweighed by the foreseen advantages. So the company started its existence.

The first actions were mainly administrative. The corporate staff was led by John Barber, who had been finance director of Ford of Britain and had been recruited to take up the position of finance director of BLMC. Inevitably he turned to Ford as a source of people to staff the central organisation and also as company staff for the corporation's operating companies, mainly Austin-Morris. Ford at the time deservedly had a very high reputation as being a well-managed company, with good management systems and able people. Some corporate staff members, particularly for senior positions, were also recruited from outside the motor industry. Recruitment from outside the industry brought in able individuals and fresh ideas but also slowed things down while the recruits adapted to their new environment.

Functions such as personnel soon had the strength to engage on such matters as agreeing common terms of employment for similar work in the different companies; the finance staff introduced common accounting and reporting procedures and a review and approval procedure for major investments. More quickly, indeed, than might have been expected, a reasonable degree of central control was established. However, even in the areas where action was taken, bringing commonality was not straightforward. Finance was a particular example. Common reporting systems were introduced, using Ford terminology. These reports were required from each company but each company had its own accounting conventions, which differed significantly. Thus, although both used the required Ford terminology, the same cost figure in, say, an Austin-Morris report did not represent the same value as one in a Rover report. This took a lot of sorting out and for some years, comparisons between companies could not be relied upon to be accurate.

In the years that followed, the corporate staff numbers and functions greatly increased. Soon Berkeley Square became too small and the headquarters moved to much larger premises in Marylebone Road. A new ancillary headquarters office was also opened in Coventry. By 1975 there was complete centralisation, at least on paper. There were nine operating divisions, all reporting to John Barber, by then group managing director and deputy chairman of BLMC, who also had thirteen staff functions reporting to him.

In arriving at that state, there had been changes of organisation involving the reshuffling of some of the operations into different divisions. Austin-Morris was split into three parts – Austin-Morris Division (essentially a sales company), and two manufacturing divisions – Body & Assembly and Engine & Transmission – manufacturing for Austin-Morris only. The most important change, however, was to merge Rover and Triumph into one Rover-Triumph company. This would prove a test of the values of rationalisation.

As already said, the success of BLMC essentially depended on the success of the Cars Group – and the success of the Cars Group depended on the development of a coherent range of cars, cars being produced to high standards and satisfying customer needs in terms of quality, reliability, accommodation, performance and service, and developed and introduced in a cycle that kept the whole range up to date and competitive.

Within the Cars Group, the cars produced were aimed at three different market sectors. The first group, produced by Austin-Morris, were passenger cars aimed at the high-volume market. The second group were passenger cars produced in limited volumes, aimed at the premium sector of the market and produced by three companies – Triumph, Rover (as stated above, fairly soon to be joined together) and Jaguar. The third group were sports cars, produced by Austin-Morris (MGB and Midget), Triumph (TR6, GT6, Spitfire) and Jaguar (E-Type). One model that did not fit into any of the above categories was the Land Rover (produced by Rover).

At the start of BLMC the Austin-Morris range of cars covered the whole of the volume car market with the Mini, Morris Minor, 1100/1300, 1800/2200, Morris Oxford and Austin Cambridge. There was also the Austin 3 Litre, bidding for a place in the specialist sector but soon dropped from the range. At the core were the Mini, 1100/1300 and 1800, all front-wheel-drive models.

The first new product launch by Austin-Morris was the Maxi. Development of this model was well under way at the time of the merger. Although the concept of a five-door, medium-sized car with a new engine and five-speed gearbox was excellent, the new management had severe reservations about its style (compromised by use of Austin 1800 doors) and the state of development of the new power train. The programme was delayed while a minor restyle was undertaken. However, time pressure was growing and the Maxi was launched with many unresolved problems, particularly with its new gearbox, problems from which it never recovered.

The first major strategic product decision was to move away from a complete front-wheel-drive range and develop, under the influence of the Ford newcomers with John Barber in the lead, the rear-wheel-drive Marina, in imitation of the very successful Ford Cortina. At the time, Austin-Morris engineers were working on a replacement for the Mini (the 9X), a new small engine to replace the A series and a significant upgrade to the 1100/1300. This work was shelved in favour of the Marina, to be launched in 1971, while the successor to the 1100/1300 range, the Allegro, was put back to 1973. The 1100/1300 had been a great success, with annual sales higher than those of any other Austin-Morris model. The Allegro was a disastrous replacement, clumsily styled (as the Maxi had been), with many faults and annual sales well below those achieved by the 1100/1300.

In 1975 the 1800/2200 range was replaced by the Princess 1800/2200 completing the renewal of the Austin-Morris range with the notable exception of the Mini, which continued throughout this period with the addition of the restyled Mini Clubman. Heritage models (Morris Minor and Oxford, and Austin Cambridge and Austin 3 Litre) were progressively dropped and not replaced. The number of minor variants in the ranges, particularly the removal of the so-called badge-engineered versions that had used such old BMC-owned marque names as Riley and Wolseley to identify 'upmarket' versions of a car, was also reduced. A note on this: 'badge engineering' got a very poor reputation through unjustified journalistic attacks. In reality it was a very sensible way of differentiating 'upmarket' versions of a model range, a practice that all manufacturers used, and much more satisfying than describing them as 'hi-line' or similar.

By 1975 the Austin-Morris range of cars was Mini, Allegro, Marina, Maxi and Princess. This was certainly a tidier range than in 1968, but the rear-wheel-drive Marina, at best a barely adequate model, had diverted technical resources from concentrating on front-wheel-drive models and was too close to the Allegro in its market positioning to provide proper coverage of the medium-size market sector. This situation was made worse by Austin-Morris, which had developed into a very independent-minded company (the many ex-Ford people in the company having apparently forgotten the Ford virtues of corporate control, or who were perhaps enjoying a newfound freedom), insisting on pricing the two models at the same level. The Maxi had too many faults to add any real strength while taking up scarce development resources. So, in summary, the 1975 Austin-Morris model range was part-rationalised but overall weak with the Mini getting old, the Allegro much poorer than the outstanding model, the 1100/1300, that it replaced, the rear-wheel-drive Marina being out of place and barely competitive, the Maxi quite inadequate and the Princess, while an improvement on the 1800/2200, not fully competitive. One big weakness, common to all the models, was the low standards of quality and reliability.

Although part of the Specialist Car Division, Triumph's highest volume product in 1968 was the Herald, a rear-wheel-drive car competing with Austin-Morris's 1100/1300. In 1965 Triumph had introduced a new front-wheel-drive car, the Triumph 1300. This car was well specified and expensive to produce, and established a niche for a small premium car alongside the executive Triumph 2000. However, the market for the new 1300 was not large enough for its volume to replace the Herald. As a result, Triumph was working on a simpler, cheaper rear-wheel-drive car, the Toledo, using many parts and body panels from the 1300. Despite the Toledo's similarity to the Morris Marina – both similarly priced and sized 1300 saloons – the programme proceeded. The Herald was dropped shortly after the Toledo was launched in 1970. A further later rear-wheel-drive model was also under development at Triumph. The Dolomite shared much of the body with the Toledo, including the doors which dated from 1965, but had newly engineered four-cylinder 1850/2000cc sporting engines and a premium interior. The Dolomite was launched in 1972 as a direct competitor to the increasingly successful BMW 1602/2002 models, the forerunners of the hugely successful BMW 3 Series. Subsequently the Dolomite range was expanded, with 1300 and 1500 models eventually replacing the Toledo in 1976.

Triumph also produced sports cars. Immediately after the merger the TR6 was launched. This model, a re-bodied version of the TR5A, was the most successful Triumph sports car, selling strongly in the US alongside the smaller Spitfire. Also under development at the time of the merger was a larger and more luxurious sports car derived from the Triumph 2000 saloon, the Stag. This car featured a completely new 3-litre V8 engine, which was the predecessor of the larger four-cylinder engines in the Dolomite. The Stag was launched in 1970 to some acclaim, but serious engine failings completely marred its reputation. It had to be withdrawn from the US shortly after its introduction and it ceased production after a relatively short life of six years.

In spite of Triumph's considerable product activity, production volumes fell. By 1975 Triumph was producing 20 per cent fewer vehicles than in 1967.

From the outset of BLMC, the Specialist Car Division faced the problem of models in one company competing with those in another. This was most clearly the case between Triumph and Rover, with the Triumph 2000 range competing directly with the Rover 2000 range. Less directly, the 3.5-litre Rover Coupé competed with the larger Jaguars. In fact, Rover had under development a model, the P8, designed to compete directly with Jaguar.

A meeting was held between Mike Carver, the corporate staff member responsible for coordinating product development, and Sir William Lyons (Jaguar), Sir George Farmer (Rover) and Mr Cliff Swindell (Triumph) to discuss these issues. Contrary to his fears, all were understanding and cooperative and it was agreed that the companies needed to develop plans in consultation with the corporate staff to arrive at a coordinated Specialist Car range of products. This was done with Jaguar moving further upmarket, Rover and Triumph combining and developing one model, SD1, to replace the Triumph and Rover 2000 saloon ranges and to fit below this a smaller model Triumph (SD2).

When the Rover and Triumph companies were combined to form Rover-Triumph, planning for the single model to replace both the Triumph 2000 and the Rover 2000 was started. It was clear that to meet the market needs for an executive car, the new model needed to be somewhat larger than either the existing Rover or Triumph models. It was desirable, too, for the sake of power and refinement, to use a six-cylinder engine instead of the

Rover four-cylinder. Thus a new six-cylinder engine was developed and with it a new gearbox. The one thing that could not be afforded was a new larger engine, so the Rover 3500 V8, although seen as less than ideal, had to be retained.

The work on designing the car went ahead smoothly enough. However, the BLMC corporate staff ruled that the production capacity should be set at 150,000 a year – far higher than the Rover-Triumph staff had forecast. This forecast meant that a new assembly plant would be required, the existing one at Solihull being too small. The new investment did not end there. A new paint plant was agreed as well as the new assembly plant. Thus the SD1 programme became an example of complete rationalisation – two companies made one; two model ranges made one; one new engine replacing two existing engine ranges, one new gearbox replacing two; one new assembly plant with one new paint plant and production set at a figure higher than the combined volume of the existing ranges.

Rover-Triumph then went on to plan the smaller Triumph (SD2) to replace the Dolomite. Following the strong advice of product engineering, this was planned as a rear-wheel-drive model in spite of the advantages of front-wheel drive for cars of this size, a matter on which the planning staff were overruled.

For Jaguar, 1968 had been the year of the introduction of the Series 1 XJ6 range of saloons – XJ6 2.8, XJ6 4.2 and Daimler Sovereign 2.8 and 4.2. The Daimler DS 420 Limousine was also introduced in that year.

Somewhat to the surprise of the corporate staff members involved, Jaguar turned out to be the most cooperative company to deal with. This was partly the result of the initial high-level meeting with the three specialist company bosses referred to earlier, but the Jaguar managing director, Lofty England, and the three most senior product engineers, Walter Hassan, Bob Knight and Harry Mundy, gave a lot of time to discussions about the future Jaguar model range and accepted the corporate proposal that the top of the range should be moved upmarket (and appropriately priced) and that the XJ6 short-wheelbase version should be discontinued. This had the effect of moving the Jaguar models a little further upmarket from the coming SD1. The Series 2 versions of the range were introduced in 1973.

As for sports cars, at the start of 1968 Austin-Morris was producing the MG Midget, MGB and MGB GT; Triumph the Spitfire, GT6 and TR5A; and Jaguar the E-Type. Triumph introduced the TR6 in 1969 and the Stag in 1970. It was decided that there were resources for only one new 'small' sports car to replace the MG models and the Triumph models (except the Stag). It was also decided that the project to replace the E-Type at Jaguar should start.

Austin-Morris, Rover-Triumph and corporate staff were involved in the discussions about the new 'small' sports car : MG or Triumph? Front engine, rear-wheel drive (like all the existing ones) or something seen as more modern – rear-engine? A delegation of senior engineers, marketeers and planners made a tour of the USA, talking to the American company, dealers, journalists, customers and anybody else with authoritative opinions on the best type of replacement for the US – by far the largest sports car market. To the surprise of many in the delegation, overall opinion was strongly on the side of a front-engine, rear-wheel-drive configuration and use of the Triumph, not MG, brand.

So the Triumph TR7 was developed as something of a joint project between Austin-Morris and Triumph – Austin-Morris responsible for the styling with Rover-Triumph engineers responsible for the rest of the work

The TR7 was put on sale in the US market in January 1975. The GT6 ceased production at the end of 1973, and the TR6 in the autumn of 1975 (except for US versions, which carried on until 1976). The Stag continued until 1977 and the Spitfire until 1980.

Before the development of the TR7 started, US safety regulations planned to ban 'soft-top' cars of any sort. Thus the TR7 was designed and initially produced as a hard-top. However, the BLMC US company made strenuous representations that the banning of soft-tops was in restraint of trade and won their case. This gave the MG cars a new lease of life and they were able to continue in production. At Jaguar the E-Type was replaced by the coupé XJS in 1975.

Thus by 1975 there was still a rather wide range of sports cars: MG Midget, MGB, MGB GT, Triumph Spitfire, TR7 and Stag and the Jaguar XJS. It was not until 1980 that the planned reduction to one 'small' sports car (TR7) plus the Jaguar XJS was to happen

The Land Rover was one of the most important vehicles in the whole BLMC model range, although this was not recognised at the time. Indeed the Rover company itself was cautious about the vehicle. If the order book fell below about one year's production, the company became genuinely worried that a decline was setting in. There was some justification for this concern since the market for four-wheel-drive vehicles was growing fast and competitors were producing vehicles more refined, more user-friendly and cheaper than the Land Rover.

By 1968 the Land Rover Series II was being produced in 88, 109 and 110-inch wheelbase versions with many minor variations, and under development was the vehicle that became the Range Rover. Originating from a study into the needs of the leisure market, the Range Rover was launched in 1970, in a three-door version with split opening tailgate, manual gearbox, no power steering and vinyl seats, a plastic dashboard and rubber mats designed for easy washing down. This was far from what was required of a leisure vehicle, particularly the lack of four passenger doors. However, Rover Engineering strongly resisted the proposal to change to, or even to add, a four-door configuration, to the extent that this work was eventually given to an outside company and the vehicle not introduced until 1981.

One of the main areas where rationalisation can yield significant benefits is in engine manufacture. Unit product cost is closely linked to scale of production. Engineering development and the installation of new manufacturing plants are major investments. All of today's motor manufacturers attempt to share engines across brands. This was not the case at BLMC. If anything, in the first seven years, engine complexity increased. Five engines were run out: the Austin-Morris six-cylinder C series, the Triumph six-cylinder OHV, the Rover four-cylinder OHC and two very low-volume V8 Daimler engines. However, five completely new engines were introduced: the Austin-Morris E series four- and six-cylinder, the Triumph slant four, the Triumph six-cylinder OHC, the Triumph V8 and the Jaguar V12. At the same time, the oldest and highest volume engine, the Austin-Morris A series, remained in production virtually unchanged.

Just as BLMC had, from its origins as a group formed by bringing different companies together, a wide range of products and models, so it had many factories, not only in the United Kingdom, although that was its main manufacturing base, but also spread throughout the world. The main UK car assembly plants were:

Austin-Morris	Longbridge (Birmingham), Cowley (Oxford)
Rover	Solihull
Triumph	Canley (Coventry), Speke (Liverpool)
Jaguar	Browns Lane (Coventry)

In addition, each company had various ancillary factories.

Manufacturing standards in such matters as productivity and the quality and reliability of the vehicles were low – in 1968 well below the best and not improving at all. Meanwhile the rest of the world, led by the Japanese companies, was setting higher and higher standards. The need for improvement was recognised, but on productivity especially, as has been said earlier, any improvements were near-impossible with the state of industrial relations that then existed. The result was that no effective action was taken to improve standards in manufacturing.

In fact, little was done to improve the state of industrial relations, except for one action – the existing piecework payment system was replaced by a 'measured day-work' system. This was a step forward but had little immediate effect – the multiplicity of bargaining units remained, improvements remained near-impossible to introduce and indeed productivity decreased for a time. The problems were partly recognised, but it seemed to be beyond the capabilities of the management to tackle them.

Perhaps the most notable feature concerning manufacturing during the period was the lack of action over the need to reduce manufacturing infrastructure as the volume of production dropped – as it did in this period. The effect was that factories were underused but the costs remained much the same, contributing greatly to the corporation's increasing financial problems.

The following table shows the car and Land Rover production in 1968 and 1975:

	1968		1975	
	Saloons	Sports	Saloons	Sports
Austin-Morris	608,021	38,838	408,365	39,562
Triumph	101,739	37,072	46,108	33,082
Rover	36,678	–	14,800*	–
Jaguar	16,079	7,072	20,517	1,245
Land Rover	46,187	–	52,681	–
Range Rover	–	–	10,585	–
Total	808,704	82,982	503,056	73,889

*reduced by the changeover requirements of SD1

The loss of production was entirely in Austin-Morris and Triumph saloon cars, which had dropped by 36 per cent in the seven years, in spite of six new models: Maxi (1969), Marina (1971), Dolomite (1972) – all additional models – and Toledo (1970), Allegro (1973), Princess (1975) replacing existing models. So much for the new models selling in higher volumes than those that they replaced. This was the core of the disaster and the cause of the loss of profits shown in the next section.

Inevitably, the financial state of the company also deteriorated. The figures used in this section are for BLMC as a whole – separate, comparable figures for the Cars Group by itself are not available although it was by far the biggest constituent of the whole. In fact the total figures disguise the extent of the car losses – the volume drop in those years was, as demonstrated above, over one-third. In 1969 the profitability of the company remained much as it had been in 1968 when the group was formed. As stated earlier, the profits were not satisfactory for a company with a turnover of around £1 billion, but an immediate improvement had not been expected. It was also perhaps a little early for signs of the expected benefits of rationalisation to be showing themselves by 1970 – and none were visible:

	Financial Year		
	1968	1969	1970
Turnover (£ million)	974	970	1,021
Trading Profit (£ million)	45	46	14
Profit after Tax (£ million)	20	21	2

Thereafter, although there were minor revivals, the group's financial position did not improve and it became clear that without help (inevitably from the government) it was unlikely to survive. The government was made aware of the position early and was kept informed of how things were going.

	Financial Year			
	1971	1972	1973	1974
Turnover (£ million)	1,177	1,281	1,564	1,595
Trading Profit (£ million)	46	41	58	19
Profit after Tax (£ million)	18	21	28	(7)

The government was faced with a choice. If left to itself, BLMC would almost certainly fail, and thousands of jobs would be lost. On the other hand, to support the company was a big move of doubtful industrial merit. However, it was a Labour government and at that time it had no reservations about taking important companies into government ownership.

It was decided to set up a committee to examine the position and to make recommendations. So, on 18 December 1974, it appointed a team 'to conduct, in consultation with BLMC and with trade unions an overall assessment of BLMC's present situation and future prospects'. The team reported back on 26 March 1975.

The report and what followed are described in the next chapter.

New Models Under Development when BLMC Was Formed

The Triumph TR6 was launched in 1969 and became the highest-selling Triumph sports car.

The Range Rover, designed as a utility off-road vehicle, was launched in 1970 and later became a luxury icon.

Triumph Stag sports coupé was derived from the Triumph 2000 saloon, but was let down by its new V8 engine.

The Austin Maxi, a five-door, front-wheel-drive launched in 1969, was brilliant in concept but flawed in execution.

The XJ6 was launched in 1969 and became an outstanding success. The 1974 XJ6 coupé is shown here.

2

The Ryder Report – Two More Years of Failure: 1975–77

The team appointed to look into the state of BLMC was headed by Sir Don Ryder (later Lord Ryder), who had been the chairman and chief executive of Reed Group during a very successful period of expansion and was now the government adviser (designate) on industrial matters. He was shortly to become head of the newly formed National Enterprise Board. The team members were:

R.A. Clark	Chairman, Hill Samuel
S.J. Gillen	ex-Chairman, Ford of Europe (just retired), US citizen
F.S. McWhirter	Accountant
C.H. Urwin	Deputy General Secretary, Transport and General Workers' Union

Each member of the team had his own advisers. The team's secretary was a civil servant, Peter Gregson (later Sir Peter Gregson, Permanent Secretary at the Department of Trade and Industry).

The team was appointed 'to conduct, in consultation with the Corporation and trade unions, an overall assessment of the British Motor Corporation's present situation and future prospects, covering corporate strategy, investment, markets, organisation, employment, productivity, management–labour relations, profitability and finance and to report to the Government'.

During the next three months the team did what was to be expected. They studied documents; they visited most BLMC establishments and listened to many presentations of what the various companies and divisions in BLMC believed should be done; and they met representatives of trade unions, BL shop stewards and staff representatives and received representations from many organisations and individuals with a relevant interest in BLMC.

It was at a meeting with Austin-Morris, Rover-Triumph and Jaguar staff concerning product plans that one of the principals of the Ryder team asked the staff present to put forward a realistic product plan representing what the company would like to do if funds were available to carry it out. This was provided, and with little revision was adopted as the Ryder team's car product plan. There was, of course, discussion and justification for individual programmes; in essence, however, the Ryder team accepted the BLMC plan for car products with only minor changes.

It seems to have been thought by various commentators that BLMC in some way deceived the Ryder team and inflated their plans above what they knew to be realistic, in order to maximise the amount of funding to be provided by the government. This is not true. The plan put forward was based on divisional plans, which the divisions themselves believed would be successful. If adjustments were made it was in the process of consolidation of divisional plans into one corporate plan, but these would have been minor, and essentially the plan for the car model range put to the Ryder team was one that BLMC executives believed was realistic and achievable.

In addition to this product plan, the Ryder team made a review of the group's prospects and those of the vehicle industry generally and came to its major conclusion that BLMC should continue as a producer of cars, both 'volume' and 'specialist', as well as trucks and buses and of the miscellaneous products, at least for the time being, that were the responsibility of the Special Products Division.

It concluded that there needed to be an extensive programme of rationalisation both in products and manufacturing facilities, and, particularly for cars, an improvement in standards of quality and reliability – in this regard it suggested that the 'volume' car standards needed to rise to those of the 'specialist cars'. It also called for all BLMC car models to have sufficient distinction to give them a competitive edge – rather more easily said than done, especially taking account of the obvious weaknesses shown up by the recent introductions. The team made no recommendations at all on how this was to be done.

In its review of the financial history of the group, the team said that the main point that emerged was that profits before tax had been inadequate since the BLMC formation and, even then, most of that profit had been paid out in dividends. Further it said that capital expenditure had been completely inadequate. It said that a big factor in this was that the depreciation charge, although it was on a conservative accounting basis, had been inadequate because a lot of the assets, due to their age, had already been fully depreciated.

On the organisation of the group it was proposed that it be divided into four profit centres to be called:

British Leyland Cars
British Leyland Trucks and Buses
British Leyland International
British Leyland Special Products

There should be a non-executive chairman with a chief executive fully responsible for the operation of the whole group

On the internal organisation of Leyland Cars, the report said that it had been decided to amalgamate all the car operations into a single entity in order to achieve the maximum possible integration of engineering, production and marketing. The team said that they realised the value of the specialist cars (Rover/Triumph staff had submitted a paper setting out the reasons for separation of specialist cars from volume ones), but believed that an amalgamated operation was to be preferred.

The team concluded that the company would require funding of at least £900 million from external sources by the end of September 1978. Of this, about £200 million could be raised by the company from current overdraft facilities. The rest would have to come from the government. It was proposed that this be provided in the form of:

£200 million   New Equity Capital
£500 million   New Long-term Loan

It was suggested that the loan be provided in stages: 1976 (£100 million), 1977 (£200 million) and 1978 (£200 million). These loans should be dependent on evidence of adequate improvement in productivity from the improvement in relations with the workforce.

It was also forecast that a further £500 million would be required between the end of September 1978 and September 1982. The form in which this would be needed could not be decided at present but the government should be prepared to provide this sum at that time.

The report emphasised the importance of improving industrial relations, saying that however much rationalisation was done, however much investment was made, the company's success depended on the working standards of its employees. It looked for significant benefits in productivity from this improvement; during the eight years to the end of 1982, a contribution of £400 million had been assumed to come from this one area – nearly one-quarter of the forecast profit before interest and tax for the period. The means by which the improvement would be achieved was through the setting up of a form of industrial democracy, with the workforce involved in major decisions. The team saw this as entirely feasible and a move that would produce the forecast results – and indeed, that bigger gains might be achieved. It did, however, warn that failure to achieve the improvement would put the whole future of BLMC in jeopardy.

Since the government would, through the injection of the £200 million of new equity, become the dominant shareholder in the company, an offer should be made to purchase the existing shares. The suggested price would be the equivalent of a price of 10p for each existing ordinary share of 25p.

The main recommendations of the report were accepted by the government and the vast majority of existing shareholders accepted the offer to buy their shares. However, a small minority would not sell and because of this the company remained a public company with the need to conform to the statutory requirements such as holding Annual General Meetings – often to be lively affairs with the minority private shareholders well-represented and mostly anxious to express their dissatisfaction about what had been done and what was being done.

The government decided not to take direct control of the company – now to be called British Leyland Limited. Instead it vested 'control' in the newly formed National Enterprise Board of which Sir Don (later Lord) Ryder was appointed Chairman. The main function of the NEB was to develop British Industry generally, but it was also given two industry 'lame ducks' – British Leyland and Rolls-Royce Engines – to 'supervise' on behalf of the government. Mike Carver was taken from British Leyland to become head of the British Leyland staff at the NEB.

'Supervision' by the NEB on behalf of the government has been interpreted by various authors and commentators as detailed control over the company's actions. A company cannot have two managements so this was never contemplated. In the situation that the NEB was in, 'supervision' is exercised by trying to ensure that the company's main actions (major investments, policies, plans) and above all, financial results, are in line with agreed policies and objectives. If the company fails to achieve adequate results, in the end the sanction is to change the company board and senior management, and not to try to interfere with day-to-day actions.

Thus the 'controlling' authority is required to approve major (above an agreed level) investments, annual budgets, long-term plans and major policies. To do this efficiently requires regular discussion between the two parties if problems and delays are to be avoided. This is clearly difficult; a tiny staff (three in the NEB case), even of people experienced in the motor industry, cannot do more than raise major issues and, if the company is not willing to listen, it can do little until results demonstrate that the company is not performing to acceptable standards and that major changes are required.

That is some of the theory about control. Turning to the actual events, the new board of the company consisted of:

Sir Ronald Edwards	Chairman (later Sir Richard Dobson)
A. Park	Chief Executive
D.J. Whittaker	MD British Leyland Car Company
R. Ellis	MD British Leyland truck and Bus Company
D.R.G. Andrews	MD British Leyland International Company
J.D. Abell	MD British Leyland Special Products Company
J.P. Lowry	Director Industrial Relations and Personnel
G.A. Wright	Finance Director
Sir Robert Clark	Non-Executive
J.A. Gardiner	Non-Executive
Lord Greenhill	Non-Executive
Ian MacGregor	Non-Executive
R.J. Lucas	Company Secretary

It is reasonable to say that a primary oversight of the Ryder Report was the failure to recognise that the poor BLMC performance was to a significant extent one of the management at formation being handed a very difficult task indeed – one which was likely to be beyond the capabilities of any management team available at that time.

One other weakness in the report was a lack of attention to how the improvement in operating performance would be achieved. The report recognised the need to improve performance – especially on costs, productivity and quality and reliability of products. Instead, the report seemed to assume that these improvements would come naturally from more investment and better industrial relations. Past underinvestment was explicitly stated as a major cause of BLMC's problems, as was the state of its industrial relations. The former would be rectified by the provision of new funding and the second by 'moves to industrial democracy'. All in all, many of the words used in the report paid lip service to the need for change and performance improvements but did not start to recognise the sort of changes needed to bring about the immense cultural transformation necessary to make BLMC truly competitive.

As a result of these weaknesses of perception, it was certain that the reorganised company faced a big struggle if the results forecast in the Ryder Report were to be achieved.

On products, the development of the SD1 continued throughout 1975 and 1976. And the V8-engined version of the model was launched in June 1976 with the six-cylinder versions to follow in October 1977. The model was very well received, but its many quality and reliability faults quickly became apparent and sales never started to reach the production capacity installed nor even to equal the combined volumes of the predecessors. In fact this was to be another failure equal to that of the Allegro in its consequences for the company's future.

The Princess 1800/2200 models were launched in 1975, taking the place of the Austin/Morris 1800/2000 range. At least this was a slight, if only slight, improvement, although it suffered from its extreme wedge-shaped and clumsily executed styling and the usual high level of faults.

The Triumph TR7 sports car was launched in 1975, taking the place of the Triumph TR6. This had been designed to be the only medium-to-small sports car, but a change in the US laws extended the life of the MGB and the two continued side by side.

Before the Ryder Report, Austin-Morris had been working on a new small car, ADO 74. This was intended to be a full competitor to the new generation of European small cars epitomised by the Ford Fiesta and the VW Polo. The Mini would continue to sell alongside ADO 74. The new Leyland Cars management decided that a new small car was the first new model priority but changed the concept completely. The new vehicle, ADO 88 (eventually launched as the Metro), would be smaller than the competition and use Mini-based components including the A series engine and transmission, to achieve excellent interior space. It was expected that this concept would replace the Mini, but it was over ADO 88 that a dispute with the NEB occurred, illustrating the difficulties that have been referred to. The NEB represented to the company that resources would be better used in developing a new mid-size car, replacing the Allegro and Marina, rather than a small one. The Mini, although very old, was still strong, while the medium sector was very weak and rapidly getting weaker. The company refused to discuss the matter. As will be seen, this resulted in a long gap in new model introductions that required involving outside resources (Honda) to make it manageable.

The main event relating to manufacturing was that the SD1 plant at Solihull was completed and production of the 3500cc model started there in 1976. However, problems quickly developed with the new paint process and the paint plant had to be changed. As already said, the volumes failed to get anywhere near the over-optimistic forecasts, but the plant was allowed to continue in this period, with no attempt to reduce capacity.

On industrial relations, the new arrangements for industrial democracy were tried and some of the committee meetings were held. However, they ran into the inevitable problem that those plans which involved new investment and increases in the workforce were easily agreed but those, equally or even more important, requiring retrenchment, e.g. to reduce capacity to match the much lower volumes now needed, were always refused by the union representatives. Eventually, the attempt faded away.

There was, however, one important action agreed between the unions and BL management. This was to change the union bargaining arrangements in Cars from the existing fragmented system to one centralised system covering the whole of Cars. This at least was a step in the right direction.

As to the financial results of the period, in the first year of implementing the Ryder Plan, they showed an improvement, substantially due to currency movements. This made it difficult to convince Lord Ryder and BLMC executives that there were problems with the underlying performance of the company. In the NEB staff's eyes, for instance, the company was taking much too optimistic a view of sales in its budget and plan for the coming years. The company argument for this was that production would become much steadier, therefore deliveries to customers would improve and by itself this would increase sales to profitable levels. These arguments were being put forward by experienced, mainly ex-Ford executives, but to the NEB staff they sounded ridiculously optimistic. Why would production become steadier? The impractical industrial democracy scheme? What about the disastrously poor products like the Allegro? However, they did not succeed in changing the BLMC view.

Shortly afterwards there came a graphic illustration of the fragility of the BLMC position. The toolmakers at Cowley went on strike and brought car production to a virtual standstill. The strike in itself was estimated to have cost 50,000 vehicles and £100 million in revenue, although such losses are notoriously difficult to evaluate precisely. Perhaps more important, it brought to an end the optimistic assumptions about BLMC's future success.

The whole future of BLMC was reviewed and the uncertainties about performance were accepted. Although the broad lines of the Ryder report strategy were supported, capital expenditure on certain proposals such as investments in new foundries and expansion of bus operations was cancelled, and further expenditures were made subject to special review and approval by the NEB – a decision that made various senior executives in BL extremely unhappy.

The results for the period to the end of 1977 were:

	15 months to Dec 1976*	12 months to Dec 1977
Turnover (£million)	2,892	2,602
Trading Profit (£million)	118	57
Profit/(Loss) after Tax (£million)	47	(5)

*to bring financial year-end into line with calendar year-end

It was at about this time that Lord Ryder decided to resign and the NEB deputy chairman, Leslie Murphy, assumed increasing control although he did not officially take over until August.

Not long after the middle of the year, Murphy initiated serious discussions inside the NEB and with the government about changing the BLMC board and the top management. He put plans in place to change the board and some of the senior executives, and these were accepted. Sir Michael Edwardes, who as an NEB board member had been very critical of BL's performance and management, and had been one of Murphy's main allies in convincing the NEB board and government of the necessity for change, was persuaded to take on the role of chairman and chief executive of BL. A new era was about to begin.

New Models Launched Before the Ryder Report 1970–75

The rear-wheel-drive Triumph Toledo was launched in 1970 and replaced the Triumph Herald.

Right: The front-wheel-drive saloon replaced the Austin 1800 and was launched in 1975.

The sporting Triumph Dolomite was evolved from the Toledo and was launched in 1972.

The Morris Marina was designed to compete with the Ford Cortina and was launched in 1971.

The Austin Allegro replaced the top-selling Austin 1100/1300 in 1973 but never matched its success.

The Triumph TR7 sports car replaced the TR6 and MGB in 1975.

3

The Edwardes Era – The Start of Better Things: 1977–82

Michael Edwardes took control on 1 November 1977. His first actions centred on making it clear that the company was entering a new era. He refused even to visit the old, large headquarters in Marylebone Road and chose to set up his office with a very small staff in the BL-owned Nuffield House in Piccadilly. He had the name of the company changed to BL Ltd. These were symbolic actions but nevertheless important in making it clear to the company that things were going to be different.

The most important immediate differences were the changes he made to the board and executive management. The old board had been large, with eight executive and six non-executive directors. The new board was small, in accordance with Edwardes's strongly-held belief that small boards were essential for the efficient control of a company – it consisted of four non-executive and two executive directors. All the old board members were required to resign, with the exception of two non-executive directors, Ian MacGregor and Robert Clark, and one executive director, Alex Park, the previous chief executive, who remained for a time but resigned in December 1977. New non-executive board members were Austin Bide, chairman of Glaxo, and Albert Frost, lately finance director of ICI. In addition to the main board, Edwardes set up an advisory board of senior executives to review and recommend on all important policy matters before they went to the main board. He also set up a strategy panel to review and recommend on matters such as product and manufacturing strategies, and a management resources panel to deal with senior appointments.

As a director of the National Enterprise Board, Edwardes had regularly listened to presentations by BLMC senior executives about their budgets, plans and major investment programmes, almost always promising better times ahead – promises which he had never seen kept. As a result of this experience of unrealism, he wanted a thorough review of existing plans. Therefore, as one of his first actions, before setting up the strategy panel, he set up two teams under Mike Carver, whom he had asked to leave the NEB and join him in BL to take charge of planning, to review strategy – one team for Cars, one team for the rest of the operations. He also set up an organisation study group under Pat Lowry, the BL director of personnel, to review the company's organisation.

Edwardes's way of deciding about people's suitability for particular posts caused waves of apprehension through the whole organisation. He insisted that all, however senior, take a psychological test, as he had done at Chloride. The results were assessed by the management resources panel. The tests covered a wide range of aspects of a person's abilities. Of these, perhaps the most useful in Edwardes's eyes was the way it assessed people as being primarily suitable for line management posts or staff posts – a great change from the Barber, Ford-derived view that an intelligent person could successfully fill any post of any nature. In general, the tests showed that there were many people throughout the company with high levels of ability, but that many of them were in the wrong post. Over a fairly short period a lot of changes were made and many people left the company.

The strategy reviews did not radically change the model strategy for the car and commercial vehicle operations that had existed before Edwardes, but they considerably reduced their ambition and particularly lowered the sales forecasts. From the reviews a new corporate plan was developed. This was approved at a meeting of the advisory board just before Christmas 1977 and formed the basis for a request for government funds of £450 million to see the company through 1978.

It was on organisation that Edwardes was to take one of the two most important decisions of his early months. The study group reviewing the organisation comprised mostly senior people from the pre-Edwardes days; they were also the people who would become responsible for running the operations being reviewed. Given their background it was perhaps not surprising that all groups strongly recommended continuation of essentially the same, centralised organisation, particularly for the car operations, as had existed before Edwardes arrived. The alternative view was put to him that what was required was more separation into logical product groups and much less centralisation. As a result, Edwardes rejected the organisation group's recommendations and accepted the alternative view. He took the decision to divide Cars into separate product companies, each responsible for a limited and homogenous range of vehicles within the span of understanding and control of management. This resulted in Austin-Morris being set up as the division responsible for 'volume' cars, Rover/Triumph and Jaguar as independent specialist car companies and Unipart as the parts supply division.

The most important (and difficult) product-related decision that Edwardes took in his first few months was to change the Metro (ADO 88) styling, even though this would delay its introduction and take resources away from the very important medium car development. The Metro, whose styling had been constrained by engineering setting strict exterior dimensional targets, had achieved very poor results in early styling clinics and was in many people's eyes an ill-balanced and poorly proportioned box on wheels. Not unnaturally, those responsible for the programme (although not the stylists, who saw themselves as having been forced by engineering to produce a style they did not like) opposed the idea of substantial change. Nevertheless, Edwardes accepted the advice that to proceed with the existing style seriously risked another sales disaster. This was too great a risk to take, and the car was restyled, giving it a more acceptable shape. This required some increase in its external dimensions, although its interior size remained the same. The Metro went on to become modestly successful after an era of new model failures.

While the decisions on organisation and to restyle the Metro were perhaps the two most important of Edwardes's early months, his two most enduring legacies to BL were to come.

The first was, after a long and bitter struggle with the BL trade unions, to diminish the power of the unions and to re-establish the ability of the company management to manage the company. Although this sounds like some sort of return to the days when the workforce could be ground down, it was not so. A notable feature of the struggle was the common sense shown by the workforce in particular but also by union representatives when faced with firm and logical proposals from which the management was clearly not going to back down. These were often difficult for the workforce, but they could be seen as necessary for the future of the company. The overall result was perhaps not an ideal state of everlasting harmony but a great advance on what had existed before.

The second decision was to start a wide-ranging programme of product collaboration with Honda, which greatly strengthened the car product development capability as well as bringing exposure to Honda's highly efficient manufacturing methods and high standards of product quality and reliability.

Edwardes's actions on these two matters are described in more detail in Chapters 4 and 5 respectively.

Although the strategic reviews forming the basis of the 1978 plan had considerably reduced the Ryder-era sales forecasts, even the reduced targets turned out to be unattainable. Economic conditions too, particularly the strength of the pound, which made imports – already very profitable because of the high price levels in the UK – even more profitable for the importers and which made exports less profitable, told against the company. Financial results deteriorated and the outlook became increasingly gloomy, as shown in the following table:

| | Results for the year ending 31 December | | | |
	1977	1978	1979	1980
Turnover (£ million)	2,602	3,073	2,990	2,877
Trading Profit/(Loss) (£ million)	57	71	(46)	(294)
Profit/(Loss) after tax (£ million)	(5)	(11)	(119)	(391)

One of the first actions in response to the weak state of the company, and a first step to matching production capacity to demand, was the closure of the Triumph factory at Speke with production of the TR7 transferred to Coventry. This action was also the first major test of Edwardes's resolve to manage the company as he wanted to, in the face of what seemed certain to be fierce union opposition. In practice, the great amount of planning to counter anticipated union opposition, including incentive payments in the redundancy terms if the production was sustained until transfer, worked well. The closure went ahead with no union trouble and Edwardes had taken an important step forward. In fact, Edwardes' planning to counter opposition before it happened was a feature of his management and played a significant part in his many successes.

During the rest of 1978 progress seemed slow on all fronts, with a lot of time taken up with union disputes. Although Edwardes stood firm and progress was made in regaining management control, public awareness of continued disputes and uncertainties accelerated the decline in sales.

It was during 1979 that Edwardes and his senior managers came to realise that the business had to be shrunk even further if BL was ever to become a self-sustaining business. Another plan, this time labelled the 'recovery plan', was developed as a result of this realisation. This included the following main items:

- Triumph car assembly to stop and Triumph factories to close.
- MG sports cars to cease and the factory to close.
- Press and Foundry operations to be reduced.
- Land Rover investment to be cut back.

Even this reduced scale of operations would, it was realised, require more government funding than the Ryder plan had envisaged. The government, very reluctantly indeed, was persuaded to provide £300 million of new funding, plus the conversion of a £150 million loan to equity. This took the amount provided to £75 million above the Ryder totals. Worse was to come. The 'Recovery Plan' had forecast losses for about two years, with a return to profits later. As the pound strengthened further than had been assumed and as sales failed to rise as had been forecast, so it became clear that yet another plan would fail to achieve its forecast results and that if the company were to survive then even more government funding would be necessary. So, a further version of the recovery plan was developed.

The results of the further replanning, which projected profitability in 1983, were incorporated during 1980 into the 1981 plan and submitted to government in the autumn of 1980. The government, not unnaturally, took some time before reluctantly agreeing to this new request, but finally did so in January 1981.

From about 1980 onwards a new factor entered the BL arena: privatisation. Up to that time, privatisation had been seen by the BL board and senior executives as a highly desirable aim but one which could only be attained, either for the group as a whole (the ideal) or for constituent parts (if recovery were patchy), after the return of the company to a sound commercial state. The main objective was this recovery. Indeed, without recovery it seemed to BL that nobody would want to buy the company or any substantial part of it. Thus the board and executives concentrated their energies, even if not successfully, on recovery and were not aware up to 1980 of any particular government pressure to privatise.

It was probably the lack of recovery, and certainly the recurring demands for ever more government funding that made the government, and particularly the Prime Minister, Margaret Thatcher, increasingly disillusioned with BL. Whatever the exact reason, the government, which up to now had appeared satisfied with the BL aim of recovery first, then privatisation, changed priorities – privatisation was to come first; recovery was still important, but secondary to privatisation.

This change of emphasis and the importance that government attached to it was not initially made at all clear to BL. The first brush came over Land Rover. External advisers to the government advised that Land Rover could be privatised. The BL board still had recovery firmly in their minds. The board knew that Land Rover was about to go through a period of declining profits (as in fact happened) and that, if privatisation were to be attempted, they therefore could not put their names to a prospectus which was at once honest and at the same time would produce a good price for the company. They therefore refused to try to sell. The government did not overrule them, as they might have done later, but from that time privatisation pressures grew and the board had to accept that it must take priority over recovery.

Partly in early recognition of the reality of privatisation of the company and the fact that this was not likely to be by sale of the whole of BL as one entity, Edwardes had increasingly devolved authority to the operating companies, making them more and more able to stand as independent companies and therefore having the ability to be privatised separately. There were four main companies:

- Cars Group Ltd
- Unipart Ltd
- Land Rover Ltd
- Truck and Bus Ltd

Edwardes, in fact, did not stay to see through the privatisation of BL. In mid 1982, having stayed longer than he had originally committed to do, he left the company. His last two years saw the implementation of the revised recovery plan, and in those two years, funding was at last held to the plan forecasts, and in 1983, as forecast, the company returned to profit. The results of his work were showing through and the company had the prospect of returning to a commercially viable state, even though it was far from that state when he left.

The financial results for his last years, plus 1983, the first year with a trading profit, were:

	Results for the year ending 31 December			
	1980	1981	1982	1983
Turnover (£ million)	2,877	2,869	3,072	3,421
Trading Profit/(Loss) (£ million)	(294)	(245)	(126)	4
Profit/(Loss) after tax (£ million)	(391)	(339)	(230)	(74)

Edwardes left a company greatly changed for the better from the badly guided mass he had taken over in 1977. The company was much better managed and this, linked with the lessons and most of all the car designs coming from Honda, had improved its operational capability. At last there was a realistic prospect of funding being contained to what the government was making available. An operating profit was in prospect for the first time for five years. All these things were due to Edwardes's efforts.

Nevertheless, much remained to be done. The industrial relations gains had to be translated from the necessary stage of conflict, now substantially complete, to a more cooperative stage if leading operational efficiency standards were to be achieved. Product quality and reliability had still to be much improved; the decline in vehicle sales had to be arrested; and privatisation had to be carried out. All these things would require the sort of determined, single-minded leadership that Edwardes had brought to the company.

Post-Ryder New Models 1976–86

The executive saloon Rover 3500 was launched in 1976 and was voted 'Car of the Year', but was plagued by quality problems.

Left: ADO 74 was a Fiesta-sized small car shelved in 1975 by Leyland Cars.

ADO 88, shown here being worked on in the styling studio, was more compact than the shelved ADO 74 but was poorly received by customers.

The Metro was eventually launched in 1980 after a restyle of ADO 88.

The Austin Maestro replaced the Allegro in 1983.

The Austin Montego was developed from the Maestro and replaced the Morris Marina/Ital in 1984.

4

Edwardes Acts on Industrial Relations: 1977–82

One factor, perhaps above all others, that played a major part in the decline of BLMC, and for that matter much of the British manufacturing industry in the 1960s and 1970s, was the state of conflict that existed in many companies between company management and trade unions. It was accepted as normal that companies should operate in an atmosphere where 'management' – those who worked from offices and directed the company operations – and 'workers' – those who worked on the production line and supporting operations but also including the lower ranks of office workers – were in opposition. No company, no industry, can prosper when that state of affairs exists.

In Britain during the 1950s and 1960s the unions, representing and strongly supported by the 'workers', had become very strong. They directed their efforts towards getting everything they could for their members, whether this was for the good of the company or not. If satisfying a demand would damage the company, that was not a matter of concern to a union – that was for 'management' to deal with. Union strength grew as company managements, in those days mostly with full order books, time after time gave in to demands for the sake of peace, paying little attention to the long-term consequences of this constant process of giving way.

This is not to say that all the blame lay on the union side. The proper interests of the 'workforce' must be guarded. This requires consultation and understanding but certainly not a state of conflict and hostility. In the years after the Second World War, and perhaps still in some places, there was a strong class-related element in the relationship. Working on a production line and similar places carried a considerable degree of social inferiority, at least in the eyes of many managers. This translated into different conditions of service, different car parks, different eating places, different hours of work, different washrooms and lavatories, with 'management' in all cases having by far the best of it.

This was the way it was throughout BLMC when the group was formed. An atmosphere of conflict existed everywhere. Moreover, what might have been a relatively simple situation of dealing with one union for the whole company in a single set of negotiations was, as has already been described, made into a nightmare: first because there were many different unions to be dealt with and also because they were dealt with separately factory by factory. Then, not only were there the official unions to deal with but unofficial shop-floor bodies wielded much power in many factories and had to be dealt with also. The situation was further aggravated, especially important in relation to the unofficial shop floor bodies, because most factory work was done under a piecework system, which itself gave rise to an almost infinite number of opportunities for dispute.

Given the background attitude of conflict, with the opportunities for dispute, legitimate and otherwise, and the number of bodies to deal with, factory managers had to spend almost all their time dealing with disputes. They had little time for thinking about how procedures and processes could be changed to improve operational efficiency and if they did want to make a change this had to be forced through. Some progress had been made. By the time Michael Edwardes took over in October 1977 the Cars companies were, as described earlier in the book, operating on a day-work system and with a single bargaining unit. However, the attitude of conflict between management and workers had changed little, if at all. Changes still had to be forced through and disputes were still very frequent. It was still near-impossible to make changes to improve efficiency; much remained to be done.

Edwardes was determined to bring about change. If it could not be brought about by cooperation, then change would be fought through. He intended to ensure that he and his management had the power to run the factories in the way they wanted to run them. This may sound as if he intended to impose some sort of management dictatorship, but this was not so. The stage of regaining management control was completely necessary if the company was to function efficiently and was a stage that had to be gone through before a genuinely cooperative and participative system, which was Edwardes's aim, could be developed.

The process of regaining control was a long and complicated one, which took a large part of Edwardes's time. At all stages he was careful to abide by the procedural rules in his dealings with the unions, but he was also prepared to take strong, although always legal, actions such as the threat of 'constructive dismissal' of workers if the terms of employment were breached in a strike, to get his way. Throughout all this his utter determination to win shone through and gave his colleagues the backbone they needed to carry through courses of action and to stand firm in many very difficult circumstances. This tough attitude and the determination behind it was utterly different from what had gone before.

The first major event in the process was a meeting in Kenilworth in January 1978, where Edwardes put the state of the company, including the need for closures and loss of jobs, to about 700 national union officials, shop stewards and employee representatives. He demanded support from the shop floor before he would go to the government with investment plans, and there and then asked for a vote of confidence. The overwhelming majority supported him and this was an important first step in establishing management credibility, and even some sort of cooperation.

Another important event was closing the Triumph factory at Speke, near Liverpool. The primary reason for the closure was the over-capacity in the group's manufacturing operations. It was thus decided to transfer TR7 production to the Triumph factory in Coventry. The decision, taken by the BL board on Edwardes's and his planning team's advice, caused great apprehension to many of the old BL hands, particularly in industrial relations departments, who had never been involved with such decisive action and who saw in it only the possibility of very serious disruption and all the problems that that could bring. Nevertheless, with careful planning and the provision of fair redundancy terms, made subject to the factory workforce carrying on so that production could be transferred in an efficient way, the closure and transfer took place as planned with no problems. Perhaps of all the early moves to regain management control it was the success of the Speke closure that gave the confidence to carry out later difficult moves involving the workforce. It was, in fact, not long before the early doubters started to change their attitude and forgot their earlier reservations.

Various other problems were met with equal determination and skill, notably at that time the closure of the bus factory at Park Royal, the refusal to give in to the workforce striking at the truck factory at Bathgate in Scotland, and the settling of a dispute, through a process which included a visit from Edwardes to the factory, of a dispute at SU Carburettors.

While these events were going on, Edwardes also took a firm stand on wage terms. An important act in this was to include a productivity element in the overall settlement. This was not popular with unions, but it was essential if costs were to be kept at a reasonable level. The inclusion of the productivity element enabled the level of the general increase in a settlement to be kept at or below inflation levels, which was essential for the control of costs but also important for the reputation of the company with the government and the public. In fact, the ability of the company to get low general settlements in the deals was made easier because, at least at the big Austin-Morris factories, there was a sizeable annual 'catch-up' element added to the general and productivity elements – an element to catch-up to the level of Jaguar, agreed as part of the single bargaining package negotiated by Lowry before the arrival of Edwardes. This undoubtedly helped to placate, for instance, the Longbridge workers.

In the meantime, the group's results were poor and more cutbacks had to be made, including the complete closures of Triumph and MG, and reductions in component factories. This proposal was leaked to the press by a union official after a BL management meeting held with a few senior union officials to give them advance warning. Because of this leak the plan was then explained to a large number of trade union officials and shop stewards and also put to the Cars Council (the internal joint industrial relations negotiating body). The unions were given until the end of September 1979 to consider and respond to the new plan. On 21 September, the TGWU rejected it. Edwardes then set up a meeting with the full Confederation of Shipbuilding and Engineering Union Executive in Brighton. There he explained that unless the streamlining described in the plan took place, the company had no chance of becoming profitable. Without the workforce behind it, the plan would not work. Further, without the workforce's backing the BL board would not proceed and would not ask the government for the funds to support the plan. So, as far as he was concerned, the company would go under. He raised the possibility of a workforce ballot, but this was not accepted.

The CSEU seemed to think that, whatever happened, the government would save BL by injecting funds. They sought a meeting with the Secretary of State for Industry, Sir Keith Joseph, and this was held on 5 October. Sir Keith Joseph was uncompromising and rejected any immediate call for funds, although he indicated that he would consider proposals put forward by BL, provided they had workforce support.

Edwardes had, a few days before these various meetings, gathered the top BL executives, about 120 of them, and got their agreement to go ahead with the plan, provided that there was a ballot and at least 70 per cent of the workforce supported it. If support was lower, the process of dismantling the company would be started. The executives strongly supported the proposal, even though they were putting their own jobs at risk.

In mid October, the CSEU was told that the company would hold the ballot with or without union cooperation. In fact, against strong opposition from the TGWU, the CSEU changed its position from that taken at the Brighton meeting and issued a statement supporting the ballot proposal. The ballot was held under the auspices of the Electoral Reform Society and the results, made available on 1 November 1979, gave overwhelming support to the plan – 80 per cent of employees voted and of those, 87.2 per cent were in favour. Thus another hurdle had been overcome, management had taken the initiative and its authority, in relation to that of the unions, had been increased.

The next, and best known, episode in the industrial relations story is that of 'Red Robbo'. During the run-up to the ballot, there had been a campaign of opposition to it. This campaign continued, in spite of the strong support for the plan demonstrated in the ballot, after the result became known. A pamphlet opposing the Edwardes plan was published and issued after the ballot, signed by four shop stewards, including Derek Robinson, the senior convener of shop stewards at Longbridge. Robinson had been a thorn in the side of management for a long time, and had received a disciplinary warning over distorting facts in an earlier pay dispute. He had now, in opposing the known and balloted views of his fellow workers, whom he was supposed to represent, gone too far for management to take any more. He was interviewed by the Longbridge plant director, Stan Mullet, in the presence of the district secretary of the Amalgamated Union of Engineering Workers (AUEW) and asked to withdraw his name from the pamphlet. He refused, and was dismissed.

The immediate reaction to the dismissal was a partial walkout at Longbridge, picketing at that factory and some support for Robinson at other factories. Although some Longbridge workers forced their way through the pickets to work, the company faced a strike. Edwardes took the initiative, and the AUEW was informed of the company's determination not to reinstate Robinson and to insist on a return to work of those on strike, with those who did not do so being regarded as having terminated their employment with the company. The TGWU had in the meantime declared the strike official, although Robinson was not one of their members and although the AUEW, his union, had not made the strike official. A crucial meeting was held with the AUEW executive on 27 November. The union pressed for reinstatement, or at least keeping him on the payroll, threatening an all-out strike. Edwardes told them that if they followed this course of action, all those on strike would be told by letter that they had terminated their contracts of employment and would never be re-engaged. No union had been faced with that course of action from a big company in Britain nor the same degree of certainty that what was said would happen. Officials by that time had learned enough about Edwardes to know that he would do what he said.

Eventually it was agreed that the union would set up a union enquiry. Robinson was to stay dismissed but would be given ex-gratia payments by the company and the AUEW would instruct its members to return to work. This the members did.

The enquiry reported in February 1980. It criticised Robinson for various failings but pressed the company, because of 'procedural failings', to reinstate him. Edwardes would not do this. The AUEW prepared to call a strike. The company asked for a ballot, but before this could be agreed some 2,000 Longbridge workers petitioned against a strike. This caused the calling of the strike to be postponed, but of itself did not remove the threat. A meeting of Longbridge workers was called for 20 February to vote on whether to strike or not. Had they voted for a strike, it is doubtful that the company could have survived. Executives were not optimistic but they had too little faith. The vote was overwhelmingly against a strike.

Why was this, when even those close to the workforce had not believed it would happen? Certainly the evident determination of Edwardes, and the executives he led, not to make concessions was believed, and people did not want, in a time of growing unemployment, to lose their jobs. Further, though, there had been a growing sense of disillusionment among the factory workers with Robinson and his left-wing colleagues. The majority of those workers had a great fund of common sense and were willing to respond to leadership of the right sort. They could perceive what was in the interests of the company and their jobs. This is not to say they trusted or felt particularly cooperative towards management, but their reaction was a significant pointer to what might be possible provided the right lead was given.

Although the responses to particular IR problems such as stoppages and the Robinson episode may have given the appearance that the company merely responded to events in manufacturing, in fact a great deal of consideration was being given to a strategy for improving efficiency in factories through the reform of working practices. On 8 April 1980, a new set of working practices was introduced. These had been tabled to shop stewards immediately after the Edwardes Plan ballot result and before the Robinson dismissal.

The essence of the reform was to challenge the doctrine of 'mutuality' where any change to a work practice had to go through a long process of negotiating between unions and management. In practice, all changes were strongly resisted and factory executives spent most of their time arguing with union representatives about such changes, rather than devoting the major part of their time to running the factory efficiently and developing and implementing improved practices.

The atmosphere of argument, conflict and resistance to change was the direct opposite of the situation in Japanese factories, where all concerned worked together to introduce change and improve efficiency, even though these changes might involve changes of responsibilities. This process was one of consensus – changes were not imposed – and the Japanese system could be viewed as an ideal system of 'mutuality'. This sounds too utopian to be true and the reality is that things did not always go smoothly or easily, but the attitudes and practices in Japanese society tended to favour all members of a company/family working together for the common good. This made it possible for changes to be agreed and implemented in a cooperative way, whereas in BL, and in most of Britain at this time, the starting point was still one that assumed conflict. In using Japan as such a shining example of harmony and common sense, however, it must be remembered that in the years immediately following the Second World War, when the Japanese motor industry was developing, it too had had many bitter conflicts. The stable state there had had to be worked for, as Edwardes was doing in the United Kingdom.

The BL proposal for changing working practices had had lengthy discussion with unions. There was no agreement and a wide difference between the views of different unions. Eventually the management decided that the changes had to be imposed. This was done by announcing that all those who reported for work on either of two days, 8 April and 9 April 1980, would be deemed to have accepted the new working practices. Normal numbers attended on these days; there were no major problems and the new working practices came in – a further reflection of the weakening of union power. The introduction of these new working practices at last gave the possibility of moving towards competitive levels of productivity.

Industrial relations problems had not, however, gone away. The next major crisis came over the end-1980 pay claim. In August of that year a

Cars claim for a 20 per cent pay increase was submitted. The management offered 6.8 per cent. There was no bridging the gap, and an all-out strike was called for 11 November 1980. Edwardes was determined not to back down. Talks did in fact continue in the run-up to 11 November, culminating in a meeting between senior management and senior union officials. Edwardes told the union officials that the offer would not be increased and that he had written to the government saying that if there was a strike, he would not be seeking more government funds. Letters had been prepared for all employees, explaining the position, and were ready for mailing on that day.

The senior union executives believed Edwardes. They agreed to a statement saying that the matter would be referred back to the negotiating machinery for further discussion and persuaded the shop stewards (waiting outside the meeting) to accept this course of action. At the negotiations, earlier offers of a bonus scheme which had been rejected were resurrected and accepted, and the strike did not occur.

Problems recurred, however, over the 1981 pay settlement. Towards the end of negotiations, the unions threatened to strike unless there was an improvement on the offer of 3.8 per cent. Edwardes was not prepared for things to drag on. He feared the damage to company sales from another prolonged period of uncertainty. Thus a few days after the break in negotiations, all employees were sent a letter warning of the possibility of closure if the 3.8 per cent was not agreed.

This letter had been the subject of intense debate among executives. Ray Horrocks, the managing director of Austin-Morris, led the hardliners in favour of sending the letter, but a few others thought it too inflammatory. However, the BL board backed the Edwardes draft.

Things looked difficult. Edwardes decided to involve the Labour Party and Stan Orme, their spokesman on industry, was briefed. Then Edwardes asked for, and got, a meeting with Michael Foot, the party leader. He persuaded Foot to try to get the general secretaries of the TGWU and the AUEW to work to resolve the differences they had over representation on the BL bargaining machinery (the TGWU were insisting on having a majority vote), an impasse that was adding to the negotiating difficulties. Eventually, a BL–union meeting was arranged under the auspices of ACAS. Edwardes had little time for ACAS because he saw no room for the sort of compromise solutions which that body typically tried to achieve. Eventually, BL agreed to quantify the value of some fringe benefits they had been prepared to give and this, with the original level of wage settlement held, formed the basis of a compromise to be put by the unions to the shop stewards. The shop stewards did not agree. The main meeting reconvened, but no further proposals were found. The BL offer was finally put to a series of plant meetings. Longbridge accepted and then most other plants followed. Another crisis had been averted, again by the views of the people working in the BL factories, against the advice of their unions and shop stewards.

Not, however, for long. In November 1981 came the Longbridge tea-break dispute. BL was still bound, although the company had left the Engineering Employers Federation, to implement the previously agreed EEF 39-hour week. Edwardes was not prepared to introduce this without the equivalent productivity improvement – the company was uncompetitive enough, without the equivalent of around a 2.5 per cent cost increase. BL therefore proposed to reduce rest breaks. Longbridge went on strike for four weeks before agreement was reached, mainly involving some increase to the speed of the production line, and a smaller reduction in the rest periods than had originally been proposed.

Not only was there this new strike in Cars but a strike started in the commercial vehicle factories at Leyland and at Bathgate. The prime cause of the strike was the proposal to cut, in the face of falling markets and sales, 4,000 jobs from the total of 18,000. The union and steward attitude in Commercial Vehicles was much the same as in Cars: they wanted more investment and more jobs, not cuts. When the management started to implement the reductions, in November 1981, an all-out strike started. Eventually, after four weeks, a mass meeting at Leyland voted for a return to work, followed the next day by a similar vote at Bathgate.

In Cars, there was hard bargaining in October 1982, but eventually a two-year pay deal was agreed. This provided the basis for a period of freedom from disputes in the years of 1983 and 1984.

Most of the action that Edwardes took over strike threats and actual strikes illustrates his utter determination to restore management control – the thing that he knew was vital for BL to have any chance of future success. And he was successful, often getting the backing of the workforce against the advice given them by their unions. It is not too much to say that single-handedly he transformed industrial relations in BL and, by the example he set, to a significant extent in the UK as a whole.

5

Edwardes Brings Partnership with Honda: 1979–82

No car company can survive with an inadequate product range. Edwardes and his team quickly realised that BL's car models, particularly those in the vital volume sector of the market, were all in one way or another uncompetitive. The Mini was surviving well, but was now very old. The models introduced since the formation of BLMC in 1968 varied between being at best just acceptable and at worst (Maxi, Allegro, Stag and SD1) disastrous failures. The essential new mid-size Austin-Morris models were some years away and the Metro, developed to replace the Mini when the urgent need was for a mid-size car, had received such poor ratings at its styling clinics that it had to be delayed by about two years, so anything new was a long way off.

By far the most dangerous problem was the lack of a mid-size model to replace the rapidly fading Marina and a completely uncompetitive Allegro in an acceptable timescale. As has been said earlier, the majority of the loss of sales was in the Austin-Morris volume car business – the most important business in the whole company with the mid-size cars as its core. A similar loss in percentage terms had occurred in the Triumph small saloon range, in which for practical purposes the replacements were in the volume, not specialist market. An Austin-Morris mid-size model existed in the previous management's product plan, but under that plan its introduction date was to be three years after the Metro. The Metro itself, with the delay, was at least two years away and so for practical purposes BL's own mid-size car was away in the misty future and absolutely could not come in time to stem the decline in sales. It was also completely clear that BL's own product development resources could not be strengthened quickly enough to bring the introduction forward or, if recent history was anything to go by, develop a model of a sufficiently high standard to meet the company's need for an outstanding model. The company was therefore faced with another failure such as that of 1975 and this time it was unthinkable that there would be a rescue.

The only solution was to find another manufacturer who would be willing to have BL use one of its designs, badged as a BL model, produced by BL and which could be introduced quickly. This was a tall order; why would any company help a competitor in that way? However, the attempt had to be made and in early 1978, such an attempt to find a partner started. With the European owned companies, no satisfactory arrangement could be reached. The main reason for this failure had already been seen with Renault, with whom talks had been held about a mid-car programme in the Ryder era. Renault had been willing for BL to build one of their designs in the UK, but for sale in the UK only and not in the rest of Europe, where it would have competed with Renault in Renault's main markets. Renault's response was perfectly logical from Renault's point of view but did not provide a solution for BL.

After failing to do a deal with the European owned companies, BL turned to the American-owned companies manufacturing in Europe. For some time the talks with GM seemed promising, but a plan developed between Edwardes and Bob Price, then the head of Opel, was turned down by GM headquarters in Detroit. The next plan was the takeover by BL of the Chrysler European company. Chrysler seemed willing to sell; the Chrysler Europe products, while by no means at the forefront of competition, would offer BL an interim medium car based on the Chrysler Alpine; technical resources could have been integrated and the addition of the Chrysler sales network would have greatly strengthened the BL sales position, especially in European countries outside the UK. In the event, when a deal appeared to be imminent, Chrysler, without warning to BL, sold the company to Peugeot. BL was left with the realisation that there could be no western partner.

The only practical course left was to find a Japanese company as a partner. This had attractions. BL executives were well aware of the growing strength of Japanese car manufacturers. However, they were also well aware of the opposition from other European companies and countries which such collaboration would engender. Nevertheless, with no western option and with survival at stake, such opposition would have to be faced. A study was started to decide which Japanese company to approach.

The smaller car companies such as Suzuki were thought to be too small or, like Mazda with Ford and Mitsubishi with Chrysler, already associated with a western company. Toyota and Nissan were so big that it was difficult to see BL preserving its identity in the long term in any close association with either. There had been an early association between Austin and Nissan in the 1930s and 1950s. In 1977 talks had been held with that company over the provision of an engine for BL, but these had come to nothing – largely, it seemed to BL, because of Nissan's lack of enthusiasm for working with BL. In the light of later events – when Nissan, having learned of the proposed deal with Honda, tried strenuously to persuade BL that it was with Nissan that collaboration should take place – it is possible that the attitude of those in Nissan with whom the engine discussions took place may not have reflected Nissan's true attitude.

The decision was made to approach Honda. Honda's technology was believed by BL to be the most advanced of all the Japanese car companies. Moreover, Honda was producing distinctive front-wheel-drive cars to the highest levels of quality and reliability. This was exactly the reputation that BL wanted to acquire. To the BL planning staff members who carried out the study, Honda provided a fit with BL's aspirations that could not be bettered. Their recommendation to approach Honda was accepted.

Would Honda work with BL? BL had no great confidence that this individualistic company, which had gone its own way so successfully all over the world, would even agree to contemplate collaboration. The initial approach was going to be critically important and Michael Edwardes applied his normal determination to ensure a successful outcome. It so happened that Sir Fred Warner, who had not long before been British ambassador to Japan, and was highly respected there, was a member of the Chloride board and well known to Edwardes. Edwardes asked Sir Fred to act for BL in explaining BL's wishes to Honda. Sir Fred accordingly made an approach to Mr Kiyoshi Kawashima, the Honda president, who agreed to meet him. The meeting took place in Tokyo on 13 September 1978.

The approach achieved its purpose. A few days later, after discussions with his colleagues, Mr Kawashima replied to say that Honda would like to discuss BL's ideas, and suggested a meeting between senior representatives of the two companies.

One of the most interesting questions about what became a long-lasting and successful partnership is why Honda was even willing to entertain the possibility of working with BL. Up to this time Honda had done everything on its own, in its own individual way. It was expanding rapidly, and its reputation for the design, development and production of advanced, high quality products was such that Honda had, in the short period in which it had been producing cars, come to be regarded as one of the world's best vehicle manufacturers. The company was selling its cars and motorcycles in most countries in the world. In the USA, it had very successfully set up motorcycle manufacturing facilities with no collaboration and was considering setting up a car plant, also with no collaboration. Why then was Honda willing to discuss the possibility of collaboration in Europe with a weak company like BL?

There were two main reasons. First, the timing of the approach was good. Honda had up to then given priority to establishing itself solidly in North America. This had been achieved. Now it was thinking of expansion in Europe and here was a European company coming along at this very time, offering some sort of partnership in Europe should Honda want a partner. As to the need for a partner, Mr Kawashima saw Europe as very different from the USA. The USA was a country that Honda knew well. Honda had sales companies in Europe and a motorcycle assembly plant there, but compared to the USA it was unknown territory. Further, the USA was a single market. Europe, on the other hand, consisted of many different countries, each with its own characteristics, laws and regulations, further complicated by the moves to develop the Common Market. Moreover, Mr Kawashima, from his contacts with leaders of the European vehicle industry, perceived the hostility with which any Japanese company setting up on its own in Europe would be met.

Thus Mr Kawashima had come to believe that, for Honda to expand in and particularly to manufacture in Europe, a European partner was essential. So he thought that at least exploratory discussions should be held with BL. However, his views about the need for a partner in Europe and his willingness to start discussions with BL were not things shared by all members of the Honda Board. Even some of those prepared to accept his view that a partner was necessary believed that a German company would be more suitable than a British one. Eventually, however, Mr Kawashima won on both counts and the proposal to hold an exploratory meeting with BL was approved.

The meeting took place in San Francisco in October 1978. BL was represented by Ray Horrocks, the managing director of Austin-Morris, David Andrews, then the BL finance director, and John Bacchus of the BL planning staff. The Honda representatives were Mr Noboru Okamura (later Honda chairman) and Mr Masami Suzuki, responsible for Honda manufacturing worldwide.

It quickly became clear that the two companies were approaching collaboration from different viewpoints. BL, even with its imperative need for a particular new product, wanted to combine satisfying this need with forming a formal long-term alliance to deal with what was very clearly a long-term product development weakness. Honda, however, even though its main interest in an alliance was to further its long-term interests in Europe, was cautious – perhaps understandably given BL's by now well-known weaknesses. Honda therefore proposed a step-by-step approach, embarking first on one collaborative programme, and then, depending on the outcome of that first programme, deciding whether to take another step.

As the first step, Honda showed a clear perception of BL's needs by making the offer that BL should produce a new Honda design of car in the UK and have exclusive selling rights for that car in the EEC. However, Honda provided few details about the car and the meeting ended inconclusively, with BL, who still wanted the long-term alliance, doubtful if anything concrete would come of it. Honda also had great doubts about going further.

In an ensuing exchange of correspondence BL, as well as trying to clarify matters relating to the use of the Honda design, tried to persuade Honda to change its mind about a long-term alliance. Honda did not budge from its refusal to agree to this, but on the model itself the exchange of views was sufficiently fruitful, even though not conclusive, for BL to decide to send a team to Tokyo to learn more about the proposal. In doing this, although BL had not abandoned its wish for a long-term relationship, it had accepted that this was a lower priority than fulfilling its need for a new car.

The three-man BL team was led by Mike Carver, with Mark Snowdon, the Austin-Morris director of product planning, and John Bacchus. Sir Fred Warner accompanied the team to introduce them, to help them on their first visit to Japan and, perhaps most important, to demonstrate to Honda the importance BL attached to the visit

The team was shown a styling mock-up of the car proposed for UK production. It was a new model for Honda, the Ballade, fitting just above the Civic range, but with a good deal of commonality with that model. The date by which Honda said it could be in production in the UK fitted almost exactly half-way between the revised Metro introduction and the earliest date by which BL could introduce its own mid-size car. This timing, if it could be achieved, would just about meet BL's needs.

However, the model was not what BL ideally wanted – a replacement for the Marina and Allegro. The Honda design was definitely, although not by much, too small to meet that requirement. The team had to make an important decision. Their brief was to make a recommendation to the BL board about whether the Honda proposal was acceptable or not. Thus they had to decide whether the model, although it was not exactly what they were looking for, could be used to save BL's market position or whether the search should go on, with time getting shorter and shorter? After an all-night discussion the team members all agreed. The model should be adopted but not as its main mid-size car. BL's product strategy should be changed.

The change was to keep a 'small' specialist model in the BL range. One had been planned (known as SD2) but had reluctantly been dropped from BL's plans because of a lack of product development resources. So, although it would not be a replacement for the Marina or Allegro, the Honda model would be an excellent replacement for the car that was being dropped from the range – the small Triumph saloon. BL's own mid-car would be retained in the plan and introduced at the planned date as a 'volume' model. Even though not what BL had been hoping for, the Honda model would give BL's product range a much-needed boost at a critical time and, with BL's own mid-size car to follow, would, in the team's view, not only greatly reduce the risk of market erosion but would strengthen the market position thereafter. And if the programme was successful, a strong link with Honda would have been established.

In the team's view, these reasons made adopting the Honda proposal a much stronger course of action than either casting around further for a partner to provide the ideal model, with the delay that would involve and with no more than a remote chance of success, or, 'going it alone' after all, with the near-certainty of BL collapse. Moreover, all the team members, perhaps to a much greater extent than in some of the rest of BL, believed that more than just supplementing product development resources was required if BL was ever to become a genuinely competitive player in the world motor industry. Its operating standards, especially in product design for efficient production and in production itself, had to be raised and its quality and reliability standards transformed. A long-term alliance with Honda, with Honda standards, not just its product development strength, in some dimly perceived way being transferred to BL, offered the best possibility of making BL a genuinely competitive company. In the end, this would be more important than adopting this one model design. Honda was not, of course, at that time offering this long-term alliance, but success with this first programme would, the team thought, probably bring another programme in its wake and the relationship would expand. To agree to the programme proposed by Honda seemed the right thing to do for both short- and long-term reasons. It was a big decision.

The next day, the BL team told Honda that they would recommend to the BL board that the Honda proposal be adopted. Then two or three days were spent in establishing more of what was involved for each company and agreeing an outline plan for the work that had to be done to make the proposal a reality. Edwardes was, of course, fully informed about what was going on. He was an inveterate user of the telephone, and some of the bills between Japan and London during that week were impressive. Even so, he was so keen to hear at first hand more about the proposal and the impression the team had gained about Honda as a long-term partner, that he asked Carver to return through Frankfurt, where Edwardes was attending a meeting, to tell him all about it, rather than wait until they met in London.

Edwardes supported the team's proposal, as did the BL board. Carver was put in charge of the negotiations with Honda with John Bacchus as his principal assistant. For Honda, Mr Okamura was head of the team, backed up by Mr Suzuki and by Mr Tetsuo Chino, soon to become head of the Honda North American sales company.

The process of reaching a formal agreement for BL to produce and sell the car was not as difficult as both companies had at first feared. One of the main reasons for this was that the principal negotiators on both sides were aiming to get an agreement from which both companies would benefit more or less equally. There was a complete absence of the rather too frequent western attitude that an agreement is only a good one if your side has done the other down. Moreover, as individuals, the negotiators got on well.

Carver was pleasantly surprised to find that negotiating with the Honda team was, if anything, easier than dealing with a western company. He had been apprehensive, given the amount that even then was being written about the difficulties that westerners were bound to have in understanding and dealing with Japanese people. In the event he experienced no serious problems from what may be called 'cultural' factors. That is not to say that cultural differences did not exist or that they were not important. In this particular case, however, things were made easier by the Honda team's wide practical experience of working in western countries, the goodwill that existed between the teams and the fact that both teams were handling an industrial negotiation from a common understanding of their industry.

Nevertheless, negotiations were not simple and easy. This was, after all, an important and complex business deal, with difficult commercial issues to be resolved. In spite of the high degree of goodwill on both sides, neither was going to give any easy commercial advantage to the other.

The BL team had also feared that language might prove a problem. For this negotiation, as with their apprehension about cultural differences, this turned out not to be so. What emerged as important was the need to spend time to make sure that each team fully understood the other. This was achieved to a substantial extent by the BL team willingly, although there were eyebrows raised back in the UK, accepting a Honda executive as the only interpreter, with no interpreter being employed by BL. The Honda executive was Mr Kiyoshi Ikemi, a senior member of Honda's international planning staff. As well as interpreting, he had his own role in negotiating, and his understanding of the matters under discussion, together with his excellent command of the English language, made him ideal for the job. BL never had reason to question even for an instant the wisdom of relying on Honda for this task.

Many Honda executives spoke English, and interpretation was not always necessary. This gave rise to few problems in these discussions, but later, as meetings at various levels proliferated, misunderstandings could and did arise mainly because participants ascribed too much accuracy to the Honda participants' English and did not spend enough time to discover whether misunderstandings were taking place.

A somewhat greater problem in these first negotiations was understanding the information, especially the financial information, provided by one company to the other. This had been, and even in 1979 to some extent still was, a problem inside BL between the companies that had been brought together to form the group. It was not surprising, therefore, that a problem of understanding existed between Honda and BL. Of course, the price BL would have to pay for the use of the design and for the components and capital equipment to be supplied by Honda was clearly stated and agreed. However, the way in which Honda arrived at those prices was not clear, since there was little understanding of Honda costing systems. Thus some things had to be taken on trust. The suspicion held by some senior people in BL (generally not those dealing directly with Honda) that BL was paying too much first surfaced at this time. This suspicion expanded itself into a belief, again held by many and for a long time, that Honda was making unreasonable profits out of BL and that this was the only reason that Honda was willing to collaborate. This belief was a very significant factor in holding BL back from taking full advantage of what Honda had to offer and is further discussed later.

Carver and Bacchus, both ex-Ford finance men with experience of product costing and pricing had, with the assistance of their finance adviser, Rod Turner, naturally done all they could by making comparative checks to satisfy themselves that component prices and royalties for use of the design, were not too high. They became satisfied with Honda's prices and never had reason to believe, then or in subsequent years, that Honda was anything other than honest and honorable in its dealings with BL.

In general, progress on the agreement was excellent and Okamura and Carver were able, on 15 May 1979, to sign a Memorandum of Understanding incorporating the main features of the deal with commitments to give final agreement by the end of December 1979 or withdraw.

Since the car was to be a Triumph (the Triumph Acclaim), the plan was to assemble it at the Triumph factory at Coventry, with the bodies being produced at the Triumph factory at Speke, as was done for other Triumph models. At the time this plan was made in early 1979, BL envisaged that these factories would continue as production plants. Honda was, to say the least, not enthusiastic about separating body production from final assembly – transporting car bodies from one factory to another was anathema to them, giving rise as it did to great risks of body damage. In the end, they allowed the BL arguments that the practice was acceptable to carry the day but remained uneasy. Then BL decided to close Canley, and to transfer both body build and final assembly of the car to Cowley, an Austin-Morris factory.

Although from the BL standpoint, the closure of the Triumph factories was logical – indeed essential – it was not entirely easy to explain the change of plan to Honda. Such radical changes were outside their experience, but at least the bringing together of body production and final assembly (the virtues of which had, rather suddenly it may have seemed to Honda, become important to BL) pleased Honda very much and it accepted the change.

This change of manufacturing plan was not the only change occurring in BL that had to be explained to Honda. As described in the last chapter, the first half of 1979 saw the struggle at Longbridge with the unions, exemplified by the 'Red Robbo' affair, when Edwardes risked a strike that could have closed BL for good by dismissing, although with full and legal justification, a militant shop stewart – Robinson – who had persistently and in the end unconstitutionally opposed Edwardes's reforms. BL was very careful to keep Honda fully informed of the risks that this and other manifestations of serious industrial unrest could pose to the programme and to the very existence of BL. However, Honda showed remarkable patience and understanding, and, although Honda executives were certainly worried, they showed little of this worry to BL and did not allow it to affect their actions.

The planning to bring the model into production went on at the same time as the negotiations. The production date, dictated by the date Honda was going to start production in Japan, as well as by BL's need for the new model to be introduced at the first possible moment, was only two years ahead. This was a far quicker model introduction, even allowing for the model being a Honda design and with much work being done by Honda (and this itself added some problems) than had ever been achieved by BL before. Indeed, Carver was very careful in the early negotiations to avoid an absolute commitment to a specific introduction date. Among many things to be done was that the specification had to be understood by the BL product development staff, and changes had to be agreed to make it feasible to produce the car in the BL factories and to use UK-sourced materials to ensure a high degree of UK local content. The production facilities themselves, some of which came from Japan, had to be designed, and the new layout of the factory at Cowley planned.

The detailed agreement was finalised in September 1979 and all that remained, in Honda's view, was the formal signature. For BL, however, the situation was different. BL could not involve another company in such a commitment without being sure that BL as a whole was being supported by BL's owner – the UK government. The government, through its Department of Industry officials, had been kept fully informed, and there were no problems with the Honda agreement itself. However, there were problems over the approval of funding for the overall corporate plan which, the government ruled, had to be approved by them before BL could sign the Honda agreement.

The problem with the overall plan was that by the autumn of 1979 Edwardes had been brought to the realisation that if BL was to continue with any chance of success, the funding envisaged in the Ryder plan was inadequate. The 1980 Corporate Plan, which the government had to approve before the Honda agreement could be signed, required funds over and above those agreed in the Ryder plan. It went to the DTI in November 1979. The DTI recommended acceptance, but there were many doubters in the cabinet, not least Mrs Thatcher herself. In normal circumstances, the British government did not deal with such issues speedily; with Mrs Thatcher involved, the delay was even more than usual and it was not until 23 December 1979 that approval was given.

While all this was going on, Honda was kept waiting and the signing ceremony, originally agreed for October, kept being postponed. Although BL's government ownership and its implications had been discussed with Honda many times, and although the reasons for the delay were explained as fully as BL knew how, Honda was, not unreasonably, worried by the delay and found it difficult to understand the situation, so different was it from anything it, a company who had always acted with complete independence from Japanese government influence, had ever experienced. Their patience was, however, exemplary and at the time only the mildest hint of their concerns was ever expressed to BL.

At long last, Michael Edwardes and Kiyoshi Kawashima signed the agreement in Tokyo on 27 December 1979. For the first time, the BL representatives met Soichiro Honda, the legendary founder of the Honda company, who, although retired from day-to-day work in the company, was still lively and active, and kept closely in touch with events in the company. His support for Kawashima's proposal to work with BL had greatly helped to overcome the initial opposition to this.

After the signing, there remained the task of completing the work to bring the car into production. In spite of all the concerns, BL people responded well to the challenge. They did not intend to be shown up by the Japanese. The start of production was, in fact, slightly ahead of schedule and the car went on sale in the summer of 1981. The programme objectives for sales were fully met, the first time that this had been true for any major BL car programme.

The Acclaim became only the first product in a long period of collaboration between the two companies, with a whole series of joint models and with many other benefits to both companies that will be described later in the book. The association was eventually ended by the sale of BL (by then named Rover) to BMW in 1996 just when there were some signs that the British company might, largely through the association with Honda, reach self-sustaining levels of performance.

Partnership with Honda 1980–88

On 27 December 1979 Michael Edwardes and Kiyoshi Kawashima sign the first agreement.

The Triumph Acclaim, launched in 1981, was a version of the front-wheel-drive Honda Ballade, the first product of the collaboration.

The Rover 213/216, launched in 1984, was based on the next-generation Honda Ballade. It replaced the Acclaim and eliminated the Triumph brand.

The Rover 825, launched in 1986, was an executive car replacing the Rover 3500 (SD1). It was unsuccessfully sold in the USA as the Rover Sterling.

6

China

Shortly after the first agreement with Honda had been signed, BL began to think seriously about possibilities with China. It was clear that China would one day become an immense force in the world motor industry and no company in that industry could afford to go forward without understanding the possibilities and practicalities of operating there.

At that time, BL was in no position to embark on any extensive venture – its resources of people and finance were tightly stretched by the task of making a recovery from the disastrous years from 1968 to 1977. This ruled out what seemed to be the ideal, to establish a joint venture with a Chinese partner to produce a BL model in China. Even though BL knew little about China, it was certain that this would be an immense task, with many unknowns and, because of China's scant resources, no chance of success. But it was still very desirable to know about China and so, instead of looking for some big venture, BL instead started investigating possibilities for smaller ventures which were within its resources and which, even if they did not produce any profits at all in the short term, would provide information about what operating in China would involve and might give a foothold for longer-term development.

There were plenty of would-be consultants offering their services – 'old China hands' – and plenty of new opportunists. Whom to rely on was a difficult question. Then out of the blue came an opportunity. This was put to BL by George (by now Sir George) Turnbull, who had finished setting up the Hyundai plant in South Korea. He had been asked by a representative of a very prominent businessman based in Hong Kong if a team could be formed to come to China and advise the automobile company in Tianjin about improvements to a mid-size van that they were producing and also improve the efficiency of the factories in which it was being produced.

He passed the request to BL. This was exactly the sort of opportunity that BL had been seeking and Mike Carver, who had been made responsible for finding out about China, took on the task of meeting the request. Details were few – the van was an old Russian design, but little more information than that was available. Information about Tianjin was, however, plentiful enough. It is a very large town in the north-east of China, about 75 miles towards the coast from Beijing. It was one of the four largest towns in China with (at that time) about 10 million inhabitants.

The first thing to do was to go and see. A team of four was decided on: Carver plus two engineers with planning experience from BL and a design engineer recommended by George Turnbull. The team would go first to Hong Kong and be briefed by representatives of the company supporting the visit. The team arrived in Hong Kong on 3 January 1982, met the company representatives as planned and went on to Tianjin on 6 January.

This was an interesting time to visit China. Mao had died in 1976, the Cultural Revolution was over and there was some slight easing of the strict Communist Party controls. Evidence of this could be seen in Tianjin where a few street stalls selling local farm products were appearing in the streets. It was, however, only a slight easing and the BL party had to get used to everything being under state control. To help them, the Hong Kong supporting company had arranged for one of their associates, a native of Tianjin who had graduated as a doctor from the Tianjin Medical University and who spoke excellent English, to support the team in Tianjin. He was of enormous assistance on this first visit and subsequently through the following visits.

The visitors were greeted in a very friendly fashion. There was a welcoming and very elaborate banquet attended by many very senior party officials at which the visitors first met with the joys (and consequences) of drinking many toasts in Mao Tai – very small glasses but a lot of them.

The work started with inspections of the vehicle that needed improving and the factories at which it was produced. There was no doubt of the need for improvement. The Russian design was old and the van fell far below normal western standards in almost every respect, especially quality. The factories, too, were old, and activity was at a low level even though there were plenty of workers. Automation was almost non-existent and working practices left a lot to be desired – perhaps the worst example being that body panels were used and welded even though they were rusty. There was clearly a great deal to do.

This first visit, which lasted a week, was spent in further inspections, driving the van and similar activities designed to acquire as much knowledge as possible about the state of the operations. These efforts made it clear that recommendations on the van design and to the production set-up could be made, but it was completely uncertain how they could be implemented.

However, a very preliminary outline of a plan of action was put together. To produce a detailed set of proposals would need a bigger team than the present one, especially including more engineers. It was also clear that more visits would be required before the plan for assistance could be finalised.

During this time, of course, discussions were being held with the Tianjin officials and a document, roughly a 'Heads of Agreement' was drawn up (in Chinese and English), which said that it had been agreed that BL was willing to provide assistance by sending a team of engineers to Tianjin but that further exchange of information was required before work could start.

The team returned to Hong Kong on 13 January and held talks with the supporting company about what went on in Tianjin and the prospects of success. The team then returned to the UK on 16 January.

Other visits by BL were made over the next few months, with one engineer, a member of the first party, staying in Tianjin for several weeks. A party from Tianjin also visited the UK and was shown around factories and BL technology. All this activity made it possible to confirm the tentative conclusions made at the end of the first visit that something could be done by BL, even with its limited resources and the difficulties involved. The formal offer to send a party of engineers to Tianjin to work with the local company to produce a detailed improvement plan was put to Tianjin, subject to Tianjin paying the total costs involved and a small margin of profit to BL. This was accepted.

Then came a bombshell. Tianjin changed its policy, with no warning to BL. Instead of working to improve the existing van, it would make a much smaller van in conjunction with a Japanese company. It thanked BL, but that was that.

This was not quite the end. An attempt was made to source simple components from Tianjin but this proved impossible. It seemed that, even with the help of the Hong Kong company, this was not something that the organisation in Tianjin was equipped to undertake. Then there was a venture undertaken by Freight Rover with a different Chinese automobile company to produce Sherpa vans or at least to sell them there, but this, too, quickly came to nothing.

So, in the sense of setting up operations in China, the venture was a failure, but in respect of the original BL purpose – the need to be better informed about automotive operations in China, it was a success and confirmed the original judgment that it was not practical for a company in BL's state to use its scanty resources in trying to get into China.

The Chinese auto industry was, however, an opportunity in waiting. As late as 1985, China was producing only 5,000 passenger cars a year. The first agreements to manufacture saloon cars under licence were made in that year with overseas companies VW and Peugeot. Production grew to half a million cars by the end of the century, with Japanese and US companies also reaching licence agreements with Chinese manufacturers. Since then the growth of car manufacturing has been unprecedented. In 2009 China overtook Japan as the world's largest car maker, producing 7.3 million cars, and by 2013 it was producing more than 18 million cars, more than the total of all European countries.

7

Privatisation and Consolidation: 1982–86

In the post-Edwardes BL organisation structure agreed between the board and government, the company was split into two, Cars Group and Land Rover Leyland Group, each with its own chief executive, who together were joint chief executives of the whole company, which had a non-executive chairman.

In simplified form, the organisation was:

Chairman (Non-executive)
Sir Austin Bide

Chief Executive (Cars)	**Chief Executive (Land Rover Leyland)**
R.A. Horrocks	D.R.G. Andrews
Austin Rover, Jaguar, Unipart	Truck and Bus, Land Rover, Freight Rover

This structure had been supported by Edwardes and the BL board, but it brought problems. There were still many matters that related to BL as a whole and for which the BL board retained responsibility – such matters as major investment approvals, dealing with the government, privatisation and approval of the individual groups' plans and budgets. With a non-executive chairman, supported by only a few advisers, handling these corporate matters was not always easy.

On a more detailed level, a surprising feature, especially in relation to privatisation, was the inclusion of Land Rover in the commercial group. The Land Rover products had much more affinity with cars in terms of vehicle development and customers than with trucks and vans, as eventually became clear.

Sir Austin Bide, the non-executive chairman, was still chairman of Glaxo, and had demonstrated his management and commercial skills in building Glaxo into a then prominent position and giving it the base from which it has since developed further. He brought these qualities, as well as great intelligence, patience and calm, to this very difficult part-time, non-executive post.

The BL board had by now accepted that privatisation had to take priority over all else. This, of course, did not preclude acting to improve the operating performance of the companies in BL, but the need to privatise did divert the energies and attention of the senior executives from this purpose.

Jaguar had emerged as the best candidate for privatisation. After John Egan had been recruited by Michael Edwardes as its Chief Executive, Jaguar had made progress in re-establishing its public image as a producer of high-quality cars. Besides, the company had been run as an independent company within the Cars Group, and had been given what was in effect complete freedom to develop as a company with an independent future. BL had used part of its government funding for a new Jaguar engine and a new Jaguar model. Thus Jaguar could look forward to some years when investment would be at a minimum.

Even so, within BL there were doubts about Jaguar's ability to survive as an independent company in the long term. It was argued that Jaguar would not be able to fund or bring together the modern technical resources to develop an adequate sustainable model range or to provide competitive manufacturing facilities. Competition from technically strong companies which wanted to enter the profitable luxury car market was growing and this would make the situation worse. However, with a new model and new engine already paid for, these problems would be for the future; but they had caused BL to look seriously at an approach from GM for the company in 1981. A series of meetings were held with GM at that time, but eventually, perhaps mainly because the Cadillac division of GM came to oppose the idea, the proposition was dropped by common consent.

There were other doubts about privatising Jaguar. At that time Jaguar was profitable. Was it wise for BL to sell its 'jewel in the crown' – a point later raised by the Trade and Industry Committee? BL needed the money. Moreover, the government was saying 'Privatise'. So, the decision was made to float the company.

Eventually, after a lot of arguments about whether the whole or only the major part should be sold, and the political requirement to protect Jaguar's 'Britishness' ('Britishness' would later become a stumbling block for the rest of BL), the whole of Jaguar was floated in July 1984, with government retaining a 'golden share' with special powers to prevent sale to a foreign buyer for seven years.

The next major privatisation episode was the move to sell the whole of the Commercial Vehicle Group, except for the bus operation – Trucks, Land Rover and Sherpa vans – to General Motors. This had originated in a 1984 proposal by the DTI that Ford, GM and BL should discuss the rationalisation of their commercial vehicle operations, since all were unprofitable and there did not seem to be room for three independent companies. It would have been too much to expect Ford and GM to combine, so it came to a matter of a deal between BL and either Ford or GM. The first BL talks were held with Ford, but to BL the GM operations seemed a better fit, and Ford was dropped.

Talks began in earnest in early 1985, but progress was slow. GM as an organisation was not given to making quick decisions. In addition, GM financial information about the costs and profitability of their UK commercial vehicle operations, especially by product, seemed to BL to be very sketchy, which made it difficult to put together a sound commercial deal. Eventually progress began to be made. However, with the Westland affair going on at this time, emphasising how important were issues concerning British ownership, preserving the 'Britishness' of Land Rover became an important and difficult matter for the negotiators. As a footnote, no politician seems to have raised the 'Britishness' of Leyland Trucks – arguably at least as important and at least as British a company as Land Rover.

These negotiations were from the start complicated by the fact that the government, because they had started the process, claimed seats at the negotiating table. 'Government' rather than DTI, since the Treasury insisted on taking part as well as the DTI. Even within the DTI there were two representations: one from that part of the Vehicle Division that was responsible for BL, and the other from that part responsible for GM and other manufacturers. Also the DTI had its own merchant bank advisers. However, the extra six or so government advisers involved remained mostly quiet and did not interfere with BL's conduct of the commercial negotiations, and relations between the government departments and BL were good.

The government, however, did try to go its own way with GM to find a solution to Land Rover 'Britishness'. It tried to persuade GM to take a less than 50 per cent stake in the company and therefore leave legal control British. The BL team never saw this as acceptable to GM and it is arguable whether it would have satisfied the 'Keep Land Rover British' faction, because GM would have had operational control. Inevitably, GM, who not unreasonably saw Land Rover as the most valuable part of the deal, wanted legal control of the company and rejected the government proposal. The government then agreed that a BL proposal to deal with 'Britishness' could be used. This was for a supervisory or controlling board of the 'great and good' who would have power over those Land Rover matters that had a genuine bearing on its 'Britishness' – powers to veto proposals to move its manufacturing location out of Britain, to insist on maintaining its product development capability here and so on. It took a certain amount of faith to believe in the effectiveness of this 'great and good' control and GM did not like it, but in the end, rather than lose the deal, which was in all other respects, including price, close to agreement, GM accepted the proposition.

After a lot of negotiations, things reached the stage when the Secretary of State for Trade and Industry (Paul Channon) saw Bide and Carver representing BL and, separately, GM representatives on a Wednesday afternoon and assured the parties that, if a commercially sound deal could be finalised, the BL proposal on 'Britishness' was acceptable, and there would be no political obstacles to the deal. The final negotiations began. After two days and nights of intensive work, all details of a deal were agreed.

Then, on the Friday afternoon, just two days after being told that a deal could go ahead if the terms were satisfactory, Bide and Carver were again called to Paul Channon's office to be told that, in spite of the earlier assurances, a deal with GM was not after all politically acceptable because of the risk to Land Rover's 'Britishness'. Not surprisingly no adequate details were given to explain the change of mind, but in view of later events with Land Rover sold successively to German, USA and Indian companies, none of which raised the slightest political objection, it does seem to have been a remarkably misjudged and weak-kneed decision.

The 'Britishness' decision on Land Rover overlapped with a Ford bid for the BL cars operations. BL were told of it when Bide and Carver had one of their regular meetings with the Secretary of State to discuss progress with GM. To Bide and the corporate staff the news was unwelcome. Although the Ford approach was a clear road to privatisation of that part of BL – Cars – which was the most difficult to accomplish, the deal was less appealing in terms of commerciality than the GM proposal for commercial vehicles had been.

In the Cars Group the news was met with undisguised hostility and all the most senior executives in the group called for the immediate rejection of the approach. They believed strongly that they could achieve success and did not want anything coming in the way. However understandable their feelings, out-of-hand rejection was a course that the BL board could not take. Even if it had been tried, it would have received short shrift from the government, which, as BL's owner, certainly required the Ford proposal to be examined on its merits.

To study the deal required discussions with Ford. There would have to be an exchange of commercially sensitive information between the two companies. This exchange of commercially sensitive information, essential if a proper evaluation was to be made, was a genuinely very difficult issue. The Cars executives believed that BL would be more damaged by this exchange than Ford, and continued to fight for arbitrary rejection of the Ford approach. Eventually, however, meetings with Ford and the exchange of information did take place. To make things as objective as possible a BL board member, Brian Pomeroy, was put in charge of the BL side. The hostility of the Cars executives did not diminish, but a joint BL/Ford study team was set up, located in Ford's central London head office, to produce an outline business plan for presentation to the respective boards. However, in the end a BL decision was not necessary, since the government, having rejected the GM bid, rejected the Ford bid for the same reasons.

The privatisation process ran into another difficulty when it was decided that Unipart, the division providing a parts service to Cars, could not be privatised by flotation because its commercial prospects had been damaged too severely by the poor performance of Edmunds Walker, acquired from AE a short time before.

This left the aftermath of the GM affair. All or part of the Commercial Vehicle Group was announced as being available for sale although it was made clear that foreign buyers would not be welcome.

The only approach for Trucks came from the Lancashire Development Corporation, which hoped to attract interest from other European truck firms but in the end was not able to do so. The bidders for Land Rover, including a management team led by David Andrews, were all provided with the same information. There were many explanatory meetings. In the end, when all the bids were assessed, there was little to choose between them. The amounts of money offered were very similar, and no bidder offered synergies or other advantages that might have given the BL company being sold a more assured future. The decision was difficult. Moreover, by this time the BL board had come to the conclusion that the group was being severely damaged by all the uncertainty and diversion of resources from running the company, which the GM and Ford bids had caused and which the present bidding was causing. What was needed was a period of calm. Further, the board had now come to accept the view that Land Rover was better linked to Cars than to Trucks or Vans, and that the retention of Land Rover would in the future open up the possibility of being able to privatise a combined Car/Land Rover company with a far greater chance of success than privatising an isolated car company. Trucks were left with the group in any case, and Vans was a natural partner for them. The board therefore recommended that Land Rover and Freight Rover be retained and not sold but the sale of Trucks could go ahead if a buyer could be found. The government was persuaded, and so calm (at least regarding privatisation) descended for a time on BL.

While all this privatisation activity had been going on, the company had had to carry on with its day-to-day operations.

In product development the first introduction, in March 1983, was that of the long-awaited BL-developed mid-car – the Maestro. This was followed in April 1984 by the second model in that family, the somewhat larger Montego. These models were undoubtedly superior to earlier models like the Allegro, but were not of a high enough standard, especially in quality and reliability, to give BL the push it needed to recover from the disastrous first nine years.

This pair of BL models was accompanied by the second vehicle collaboration with Honda, the Rover 213 in 1984, to be followed in March 1985 by the larger-engined version, the Rover 216. The design was essentially Honda's Ballade with a more varied range of BL models than the Acclaim. It carried on the success of the Triumph Acclaim and succeeded that model in having BL's highest standards of quality and reliability. The Rover 216 was particularly important for Rover because it featured the first installation of a Rover engine in a Honda-based vehicle. The installation was not easy because the Rover and Honda engines were located on different sides of the engine bay, but despite some resulting compromises the Rover 216 was competitive.

Various models were discontinued in this period, the main ones being the Allegro in 1982, the Austin Ambassador (a face-lifted Princess) and

Morris Ital (Marina) in 1983 and the Triumph Acclaim in 1984. This was the last Triumph saloon and had been replaced by the Rover 200 series.

Of the other models being developed, the main one was a major collaborative development with Honda for an SD1 replacement for BL, with the Honda version to be Honda's first venture into the large saloon sector of the market aimed primarily at North America. Compared with the Acclaim programme, this was a very ambitious venture indeed, with Honda's willingness to embark on it influenced not only by successful progress on the Acclaim but also by the fact that this was a type of car with which BL had had long experience while Honda had none. The models developed under this programme, code-named XX and HX, were to become the Rover Sterling/Rover 800 and the Honda Legend respectively. Not only was the model to be designed and developed jointly, with that work to be done partly in the UK and partly in Japan, but the programme went further – each company was to manufacture the other's model. Rover was to make Honda versions in the UK for sale by Honda in Europe; Honda was to make Rover versions in Japan for sale by Rover there and in other Far East markets. Further, this time there was to be no market exclusivity – Honda and Rover versions would be sold through each company's sales networks in all markets, in direct competition with one another. In every way this was the most difficult and elaborate joint programme ever undertaken by two independent vehicle manufacturers. It is difficult to conceive of a programme which would test the strength of the collaborative ties more rigorously than XX/HX.

There were very many matters on which there had to be agreement. The fundamental specification had to be agreed; so had the differences in specification to allow the cars to be sold in competition with one another in the same markets. These specification differences had not, however, to be so great as to preclude the high degree of commonality needed not only to reduce development costs but to obtain economies of scale in purchased components and in manufacturing and also to make it practical and economical for each company to manufacture the other's car on the same production line as its own. Then there had to be agreement on who would do what – the way in which the design responsibility for the car would be divided and the joint development handled. How would differences in language and engineering and control systems be overcome? Those were only some of the major matters. Others included commercial negotiations about the split of investment costs, the prices of components bought from one another, charges for the work done for one another, how prices to customers would be set and a host of smaller matters. This was not a programme for the unambitious or faint-hearted.

Inevitably, things did not go smoothly. Honda Research and Development, Honda's product design company, though inexperienced in the development of large cars, did not take design proposals from another company at all easily. BL's product development engineers, for their part, included many who still held the belief that, with the history of some of the most illustrious marques as background, they could design any car, and certainly an executive car, better than any Japanese company.

These attitudes did not make for an easy working relationship between the product development engineers, but even had there been the most cooperative of attitudes on both sides, the task was formidably difficult. One example of things causing friction was BL's design of the engine bay, which Honda had wanted done by a joint team. This to BL seemed unnecessarily complicated and expensive, especially as Honda had only one engine to fit – a new V6 – while BL had that V6 and its own four-cylinder engines to accommodate. BL insisted on doing the work, but it was late and in Honda's view, inadequate. Then Honda changed the initial design of the new V6 engine, originally intended for the Prelude, in order to make it more suitable for a larger car, and the engine bay had to be changed. This sort of design change seemed natural to Honda – indeed to many outside Honda R&D it seemed that the engine designers' main purpose in life was to make late changes to engine designs – but BL engineers took it as a Honda failure.

At the end, the degree of overall design commonality between the Honda and the BL versions of XX/HX was less than had been hoped, but enough was retained to make use of many common components and to enable both versions to be produced on the same assembly line. This was, in fact, a very considerable achievement and a tribute to the willingness of both engineering teams, in spite of the many disagreements and the frictions between them, to make the compromises necessary to achieve the main aims of the programme.

While the design work was proceeding, so too were the commercial negotiations, the setting up of a nucleus of a joint purchasing organisation and the planning of the manufacturing systems and facilities. In purchasing, BL was to have the final say on the purchase of European-sourced components but Honda involvement was necessary because many of the components were for the Honda version of the car to be produced by Rover. Honda would not leave decisions on those components to Rover alone. The stationing of some Honda purchasing staff in the UK to work alongside BL purchasing staff was, in the event, a valuable move for Honda, preparing them for what they had to face when they started car production in the UK.

Nevertheless, there were many difficulties in the working of this joint purchasing organisation. The purchasing practices of the two companies were different. In the UK, BL tried to dictate to its suppliers, cooperation with them was rudimentary and, although some regard was paid to quality, price was the major consideration for the purchasing staff when making sourcing decisions. Even so, it was normal for BL, and other UK manufacturers, to accept an annual price increase for its components. Thus, in spite of the emphasis on price in the initial negotiation, increases in component prices were accepted as inevitable.

In Japan, Honda, in common with other vehicle manufacturers, had established long-term relationships with its suppliers, worked closely with them on design, production methods, quality and ways to reduce costs. Thus the purchased components were of high quality, right for the model in which they were to be used and with a steady cost reduction through the component's life. The difference with Rover could hardly have been more marked. The two companies worked together only with the greatest difficulty and it was in purchasing that the relationship was as strained as anywhere.

On the manufacturing side of the XX/HX programme, the responsibility on the BL side lay with Andy Barr, the BL director of manufacturing and on Honda's side with Fujio Ishikawa, later a Honda executive vice president, who had taken over the responsibility for Honda's manufacturing worldwide from Masami Suzuki on the latter's retirement. As well as his Honda corporate responsibilities, Ishikawa was also head of Honda Engineering, the Honda company responsible for the design and manufacture of manufacturing facilities and tooling, when purchased facilities would not meet their needs. This ability to produce essentially 'custom' facilities was, and remains, a great strength and a significant factor in Honda's high level of manufacturing efficiency.

Honda's approach to the type and use of manufacturing facilities was different from BL's. It was of fundamental importance to Honda that manufacturing facilities should be sufficiently flexible to allow the production of more than one model on the same set of facilities and be capable of adaption in the future for the production of new models. BL at that time certainly invested in modern facilities, but paid less attention to their flexibility and ability to be adapted for future models.

Also fundamentally important to Honda was that all production facilities should be continually improved and kept up to date, and for this purpose they listened to those operating the facilities and used their suggestions to a greater extent than did BL. It was, in fact, Ishikawa's strong belief that by far the most important thing to ensure efficient production was to involve the people operating those facilities in the way they were used. This is also a Toyota attitude: the 'Toyota Production System' sets out to involve people – to give machines 'a human face'. In the meantime, the BL thrust in manufacture was to install new facilities with a high priority given to automation. Over the years, particularly in the later years when the company had become the Rover Group, many articles appeared in newspapers and magazines about the efficiency that would come from the advanced technology and high levels of automation being installed in BL car factories. It was not until later, when Honda's lessons were being absorbed, that these benefits started to come.

As with product engineering, the relationship between Honda and BL manufacturing people was often strained. Most BL manufacturing executives did not intend to be dictated to by the Japanese over the type and choice of manufacturing facilities any more than they intended to accept Honda advice to listen to the operators. Nor did they find sympathetic the Honda way of tackling manufacturing process or quality problems. Honda's attitude was to believe that a reported problem existed and to worry it to death until its real cause had been established or, very rarely, until it was certain that no problem existed. Each established problem was listed, and the cause and solution demonstrated diagrammatically. The general BL attitude was to hope that the problem would go away. A certain number of Honda people were established at Cowley and Longbridge. Their reports and proposals were largely ignored. One very senior manager complained that all the Honda people wanted to do was to record and draw pretty diagrams. The cultures were far apart.

Further disagreements arose over Honda prices for manufacturing facilities, adding another problem to the already established friction over component prices. The existence of this problem made many difficulties for those carrying out detailed negotiations with Honda.

Honda certainly expected to make a normal commercial return on what it sold to BL and on the work they did for BL, although there were cases when it was clear to an unbiased observer that it had given very favourable terms to BL. It is difficult to understand why the adverse view of Honda's motives was so strong and so widespread. That it should be held by a few people is natural enough, but it was held by many and half-believed by others, even at the most senior level. It certainly affected the willingness of BL to listen to Honda on any matter, slowed down the process of developing a true long-term relationship and was an important factor in preventing the full potential of the relationship from being developed.

Perhaps the biggest single reason for this assessment of Honda's motives was an underlying resentment at being required to acknowledge that another company, and a Japanese one at that, was doing things better than BL. This, linked with a genuine puzzlement about why on earth a successful company like Honda should collaborate with BL if its main motive were not to make money out of the relationship, was probably at the basis of this anti-Honda feeling. This lack of trust in business relationships, the deep-rooted suspicion that the other party is trying to do you down, is a problem for many western companies and regularly stands in the way of their making a success of collaboration.

While the XX/HX programme development was proceeding, discussions started on the programme to replace the Triumph Acclaim (the Rover 200 range launched in 1984). Of utmost importance, a Honda version of the model was to be built for Honda by BL and to be sold by Honda in Europe as the Honda Ballade. Thus, as with XX/HX, Rover and Honda were to compete in the same markets.

During this period the financial results for the whole group, after a bad first year, improved but then deteriorated. The results for this period were:

	Year ending 31 December			
	1982	1983	1984	1985
Turnover (£ million)	3,072	3,421	3,402	3,415
Trading Profit/ (Loss) (£ million)	(126)	4	(12)	(35)
Profit/(Loss) after Tax (£ million)	(230)	(7)	(73)	(126)

This period of split management, with a non-executive chairman had been a period of consolidation. In Cars, the relationship with Honda had deepened and widened. All through the group the benefits of better industrial relations had been felt. However, the looked-for sustained commercial recovery had not been achieved. Correctly or not, the government perceived the split organisation as a factor in this and decided that there should be a return to a single chief executive.

The man selected was Graham Day, a Canadian, who had been chief executive of British Shipbuilders and had had long experience of working with the British government in that post. He was forceful, intelligent and energetic, and even though he had no experience of the motor industry his qualities seemed well suited to the formidable task of leading BL to genuine competitiveness and, most of all in the government's eyes, to lead it into the private sector.

8

Graham Day: 1986–88

Graham Day came to BL with a strong remit to make progress on privatisation, still the government's policy for BL's future in spite of the temporary halt called for Land Rover and the difficulties encountered in the privatisation attempts leading up to that halt described in the previous chapter. Day, like Edwardes, immediately acted to make it clear that a new era was beginning. He changed the name of the company to Rover Group plc and moved the headquarters from Uxbridge to Hobart Place in London so that he could easily maintain good contacts with government.

The previous chairman, Austin Bide, of course resigned and Day brought in Archie Foster, chief executive of Esso UK and Ned Dawnay of Lazards Merchant Bank as non-executive board directors. He also added David Hankinson, the new finance Director, and Mike Carver, as group executive director, to the board as executive directors. The two joint executive directors, Ray Horrocks and David Andrews left, like Austin Bide, as a consequence of the change of organisation. Harold Musgrove, the managing director of Austin-Rover and some of his most senior executives also left; Les Wharton took on the managing director role.

The first strategic decision that Graham Day faced concerned the product plan. Three major new projects were about to be given the go-ahead – a new state-of-the-art K series small engine, the long-awaited replacement for the A series; an all new small car code-named AR 6 to replace the Metro; and a joint Honda-Rover development of a medium car (R 8) to replace the Maestro, Montego and Rover 213/216. At that time the government had to sign off Rover's investment plans and it was clear only two of the three would be funded. Austin-Rover management made the case for all three projects, but this was not acceptable to the government. Around this time engineers had demonstrated that the K series could be installed in the current Metro by making significant changes to the engine bay. This offered a way forward and the K series engine and its installation in the Metro and the R 8 were approved despite some reservations over Rover's capability to engineer all the projects successfully.

Privatisation was quiet for a while and the most important early event in Day's reign was that the XX/HX (Rover 800/Sterling and Honda Legend) production started. The way the two companies had handled it, set out in the last chapter, illustrates the type of problem that occurred between them – showing the sorts of difficulties that arose from the different attitudes and experience of people in both companies. It is to the great credit of those involved that these difficulties were always overcome.

The models from the XX/HX programme started being sold in Japan from October 1985 and in the UK in July 1986, followed by the launch in the USA. For Honda, the main Legend market had always been the USA, and it set up a new dealer network, the Accura, to sell the car. It was a remarkable success, soon scoring top ratings in levels of customer satisfaction. The Rover model, considered by many to be better styled than the Legend, was at first well received in the UK, but this did not last and sales (as had been the case with many previous models) fell well below estimates. Then, in 1987, the Sterling version was introduced into the USA, amidst more high hopes and the usual forecast of high sales, but again these expectations were not realised and the American programme was a disastrous failure, following the equally disastrous failure of the SD1 there.

Why was the Legend such a success and the Rover a relative failure in the UK and a complete failure in USA? The main reason is clear – poor Rover quality and reliability. The 1988 J.D. Power ratings for the two cars in the USA show that the Sterling had considerably more faults than any other car in its class and five times the number of faults of the Legend, which was at the top for customer satisfaction.

Why was there so great a difference in what was largely a common design, given what has been said about the benefit of Japanese designs for production of vehicles of high quality? The quality and reliability of the Honda-produced Legends was as high as any other Honda model – perhaps higher. On the Rover version, however, Rover had insisted on its own design for many systems and components in the car. The core of the problem lay there. To Rover senior management it is not too much to say that, in the early months of Rover production, as service experience accumulated and more and more faults were reported, it seemed that every Rover design element that was different from the Honda design produced a fault. When the faults on the American model became apparent, an enormous effort was put into correcting them, but this did not succeed in getting the car to an acceptable standard. This failure is perhaps the most striking and disappointing example, among the multitude that exist, of BL's failure at the sharp end – of its failure to design efficiently for production and then to produce efficiently and to a high standard. Eventually the model had to be withdrawn from the American market.

With regard to the Honda relationship, Graham Day had, in fact, immediately recognised the importance of that relationship to Rover and had established a good working relationship with Tadashi Kume, who had succeeded Kawashima in September 1983 as Honda president. Day liked Japan and had visited the country many times and worked with the Japanese when he was working with Canadian Pacific. Honda people were impressed by his attitude and by the improvement in BL performance that they saw him bringing about. Without him, the subsequent expansion of the relationship might not have been possible.

Honda had asked Rover to produce first the Legend and then the Ballade for it because it saw this as a way of increasing its sales in Europe, particularly in those countries with import restrictions – France, Italy and the UK – since the cars would be regarded as European in origin. For Rover, manufacturing for Honda represented a chance to improve its production volume and therefore profits. It also seemed to Rover a mark of approval in that Honda now saw the standards of Rover production as high enough to meet their standards of quality and regularity of supply.

Although the primary intention of the plan for the Ballade to be produced for Honda was not to improve Rover manufacturing performance, this was eventually its effect. Although a start had already been made in manufacture for Honda with the Legend, serious quality problems at Cowley and problems in Japan, where the Rover 800 production had started, and low production volumes, made both companies decide that the sensible thing was to stop producing this car for one another. Thus the Ballade production programme was the real test of Rover's capability of manufacturing for Honda and the real start of Rover's improvement in its ability to produce products of a high quality. The design was Honda's, so the other part of Rover's operational deficiency – its inability to design for efficient high-quality production – was not a factor.

The Ballades were produced at Longbridge and shipped to the newly established Honda receiving centre at Swindon, where cars from Japan were also received. The Longbridge cars had already been inspected and rectified to Rover's satisfaction at Longbridge before dispatch. They were again inspected, as were the cars from Japan, at Swindon by Honda. Soon after production started, Honda Swindon claimed that the cars received from Longbridge had unacceptably low quality levels – in their measurement, the Longbridge-produced cars had between six and ten times the number of faults that occurred on the cars received from Japan. Many senior Rover executives found these figures hard to believe. The level of customer satisfaction with the Rover 200, produced on the same line by the same people as the Ballade, was high. Moreover, in some recognition of Honda's higher standards, the Ballade was given a more thorough inspection and fault rectification than the Rover 200. Thus in Rover eyes Ballade quality ought to be good enough for Honda.

When Honda said that Longbridge-produced cars had so many more faults than Japanese-produced cars, Rover manufacturing people claimed that Honda was creating a problem because Ballades were not selling well. There was, in fact, no evidence of this supposed lack of sales, but it was a view widely accepted in senior Rover ranks and needed settling.

The upshot was that Carver, who had under his control a technical team responsible for quality audits on Rover cars, had this team carry out an audit comparing the number of faults on the cars Honda were receiving from Japan and those received from Longbridge. This audit proved that Honda was correct. It is true that many of the faults were tiny, things that very few customers would have noticed, but it was because they insisted that everything, however tiny, should be put right that Honda achieved such high overall quality standards. The value of this striving for absolute perfection was difficult for many Rover managers to understand and, far less, accept. However, many Rover production line workers came to understand what Honda was trying to do and welcomed it.

Nevertheless, whether they really believed in such standards or not, the Rover manufacturing managers had to accept that they must meet Honda standards and from then on made progress in improving Ballade quality. Although this was mainly done at great expense by rectification off the production line, within a few months the number of faults on the cars received from Longbridge had been greatly reduced.

There was one important difference of approach to quality that contributed to the differences in assessment of quality and which is worth noting. Rover at that time was willing to accept that the dealers' pre-delivery inspection was part of the process of making the car acceptable to the customer. Honda, on the other hand, expected to deliver their cars to the dealer in a perfect condition. This argument over the quality of Ballade production was the first step towards a true realisation in Rover of the standards that had to be reached if the company was really to succeed.

Honda, although it had shown a lot of faith in Rover in asking it to produce the Ballade, had been cautious enough to make the implementation of the next joint programme, that for the Rover 200/Ballade successor, conditional on Rover achieving acceptable quality standards on the Ballade. Code-named R8/YY, it was conceived as a much bigger programme in all respects than the Rover 200/Ballade programme. The Rover models in the programme were to replace not only the Rover 200, but also the bulk of the Montego and Maestro range; the volumes to be produced for Honda were to be substantially increased.

In developing the new programme, although in theory a joint development programme, BL had recognised the problems of their design failure with the XX/HX programme. At the outset, both sides committed to avoiding similar wranglings; Honda was to take the design lead and Rover would not make so many changes to the Honda design as they had with XX/HX. The model design was, in fact, the Honda design for its new Concerto but with a different front suspension system as proposed by Rover. The programme covered the following models:

- Rover 200 five-door notch-back, with Rover 1400cc engines (new) and Honda 1600cc engines from Swindon.
- Rover 200 three-door. This was a Rover model only with the necessary design changes from the five-door carried out by Rover.
- Honda Concerto five-door, with Honda engines from Swindon.

A four-door model, to be produced for both companies, was later added to the model range. For Rover, this was designated the Rover 400 series, using both the Rover 1400cc and the Honda 1600cc engines. Later, Rover entirely independently introduced 2-litre petrol, Peugeot diesel engined, coupé and estate car versions.

Because of the improvements in Ballade quality, Honda did not exercise its right to withdraw from the R8/YY programme. It did, however, see that Rover would require a lot of help to bring the model into production efficiently. It therefore offered Rover a substantial programme of technical help. There were, however, objections to the price and many in Rover manufacturing did not welcome the programme, still believing that they had little to learn from Honda and therefore did not need it. Eventually a watered-down programme was agreed.

In the first year of production Rover ran into problem after problem and time and again failed to produce anything like the volume it scheduled for production. A re-scheduling would follow, but there would be a further failure to meet the new lower schedule. This went on for months and it was a source of concern to Honda that there could be so little realism in Rover as to set schedules that experience showed were most unlikely to be met. Rover manufacturing blamed many of problems on inadequate Honda-provided manufacturing facilities, but there is little doubt that the problems were a direct result of Rover's own inadequacies and reluctance to use to the full the assistance that had been offered.

It was, of course, not only Honda which was troubled by these scheduling problems but also all Rover's suppliers, many of whom had a financially difficult period because of Rover's inability to schedule accurately. This process was a reflection of how far Rover had still to go in developing a working 'minimum inventory' system. Suppliers were still not being properly considered as an integral part of the production process.

After about a year production did settle down and the model became a success, being recognised as an 'upmarket' model, thus bearing out the belief of those who saw it as the prime mover in establishing Rover as a 'specialist' car company.

While all this product activity was going on, in reviewing the possibilities for privatisation, Day perceived that Cars as a whole could not be privatised in the near future at anything but a very low price. He also saw Land Rover and Cars as a combined company having a greater chance of being privatised on reasonable terms earlier than Cars by itself. He nevertheless kept Land Rover as essentially a self-contained company in order to make it possible to privatise that company separately should that be a practical early step.

In turning his attention to the Truck and Van operations, Day saw an opportunity to do a deal with DAF, the Dutch commercial vehicle company. In his Canadian Pacific days he had had contacts with the financial adviser to the family that held the majority holding in DAF. Through this channel, he revived talks that had started and which had earlier produced some limited collaboration between the two companies.

By the end of 1986, the outline of a deal with DAF was in place and incorporated in the 1987 corporate plan submitted to the government. The deal required the government to write off the accumulated debts of the Truck and Bus Division and the rationalisation costs of the deal. This was eventually agreed with the EC as £680 million. DAF would have 60 per cent of the new company, DAF/Leyland. The deal was completed in February 1987, with George Simpson, the then managing director of Freight Rover, becoming managing director of the UK operations of the new company, with a seat on the DAF Board, as had Graham Day.

This deal, which was due to Day's vision and leadership, seemed at the time to senior BL executives to be at least as good as the GM deal would have been, and probably better from the point of view of preserving BL's Truck and Van operations in a viable form. The later collapse of DAF has shown that the prospects were less good than everybody assumed at the time, but it would have required an impossible degree of foresight to have predicted that collapse.

While this was going on, privatisation of smaller parts of the business was proceeding. The management of Unipart, backed by Charterhouse, revived a management buyout proposal that had earlier been refused because of BL's wish to float the company – an action which, as already mentioned, had been frustrated by Unipart's Edmunds Walker problems. Although some problems still existed, Charterhouse had been sufficiently impressed by Unipart's management to persuade city investors to back the management buyout, which was completed in 1987. Three other Rover companies were also privatised through management buyouts: Istel Ltd, the Rover computer services arm; Rover Australia, which handled Rover sales there; and later, Leyland Bus.

These privatisations left Cars and Land Rover as the only parts of Rover remaining in government ownership. Given the still poor results of Cars, flotation even of a joint Car/Land Rover company on reasonable terms, or any terms for that matter, seemed impossible. A sale to a vehicle manufacturer might be possible, but political problems could be revived since that manufacturer was bound to be foreign (the issue of 'Britishness' still existed). Land Rover by itself could have been floated or sold, but there were problems. Many in Rover, as had been the case when the company's sale was originally proposed, doubted the ability of Land Rover to survive for long as an independent company, and this would give problems over writing a prospectus. A vehicle manufacturer as purchaser would, as with Cars, be foreign and if that would provide political problems for Cars, those problems would be more severe for Land Rover. Finally, it was still desirable to have Land Rover as 'bait' for floating a combined company when Cars' performance improved to the degree that made it possible.

In spite of what its management team must have known about the political difficulties, VW expressed an interest in buying Rover cars, and some preliminary talks were started in the autumn of 1987. These had made no significant progress when the possibility of British Aerospace being a purchaser emerged. This had started in a private conversation between Sir Roland Smith and Graham Day about BAe acquiring Land Rover only, but soon came to include the whole Rover Group. BAe made this formal by approaching the government in December 1987.

Both BAe and Rover wanted the bid to be exclusive. Rover had had a lot of experience of public speculation about its ownership and knew the great damage to sales that a public auction could do. BAe of course wanted the commercial advantage that such a deal would bring. The deal which, if it could be done, met all the government's privatisation objectives and thus was so appealing to the government that, against the advice of their merchant bank, Barings, it granted a two-month period of exclusivity. This made Ford, who after the previous debacle had been promised the opportunity to bid for Rover if circumstances changed, very unhappy and they protested to the Secretary of State. The protest was to no avail.

The negotiations proceeded with a frenzy of work between the two companies, and between the companies and the government and the EC Commission. By the end of March 1988 the following terms were agreed:

- Government to provide £800 million to remove Rover debts
- BAe to pay £150 million for the government's Rover shareholding
- The government guarantee covering BL obligations to be removed
- BAe to hold Rover and Land Rover for at least five years
- Rover not to use more than £500 million of its tax losses.

Negotiations with the EC Commission over the terms went on until July and, although subsequently problems emerged, these were thought to have been fully understood and agreed. The BAe board then formally agreed to the purchase.

From Graham Day's point of view, the deal seemed the best solution to the privatisation imperative that could have been developed. This was a view shared by the Rover board and most of the senior executives. One or two senior executives supported for a time the possibility of developing a management buyout, but most did not believe that they could support a sufficiently optimistic prospectus because they did not believe that the company could survive long on its own. Further, BAe was seen as a strong company (certainly disproved by later events but a view that was universally held at the time), which could provide support to Rover should it become necessary. Although there was much talk about synergies (especially technical) between the two companies, these were not a major factor in the BL assessment of the deal.

From BAe's viewpoint, the acquisition strengthened the appearance of the BAe balance sheet by adding a large amount in assets. The chairman, Sir Roland Smith, was ambitious to expand BAe and he and his staff presumably believed that Rover's prospects were good enough to be an asset to BAe. In this regard the Honda connection was very attractive, as BAe wanted to expand its aircraft links in Japan and saw the links between Rover and Honda as a support when dealing with other Japanese companies.

Although much subsequent press and political comment rated the price paid for Rover as a bargain, this certainly did not appear so at the time, at least to Rover executives, who were acutely aware of the struggle that still existed to bring the company to sustained viability, of its cash needs and of its poor profit record, shown below, for the period preceding the sale.

	Year ending 31 December		
	1985	1986	1987
Turnover (£ millions)	3,415	3,412	3,096
Trading Profit/(Loss) (£ millions)	(34.6)	(246.4)	16.8
Profit/(Loss) after Tax (£ millions)	(125.3)	(455.6)	(21.6)

The British Aerospace Years 1988–94

Replacing the Maestro, the Rover 214, launched in 1989, was a successful Honda-designed medium car using the excellent Rover K series engine.

The Rover 100, launched in 1990, was an updated Metro, modified to take the K series engine.

The Rover 200 Coupé, launched in 1992, was the Rover-designed sports coupé derived from the Rover 214. (HMC)

The Rover 600, launched in 1993, was a restyled version of the Honda Accord.

The Land Rover Discovery, launched in 1989, was an additional model designed to appeal to the growing leisure 4x4 market.

The second-generation Range Rover, launched in 1994, reinforced its luxury status. (HMC)

9

British Aerospace Ownership: 1988–94

Within the Rover Group, after the takeover it was possible to integrate Cars and Land Rover to a far greater extent than before, when they had been kept separate in case of the need to privatise Land Rover by itself. Thus the organisation was changed to bring both companies together under one managing director with Graham Day becoming chairman, rather than chairman and chief executive. The managing director's post went to George Simpson who came back into the company, with DAF's agreement, from DAF/Leyland, where he had been highly regarded. John Towers assumed product development responsibilities in addition to those for manufacturing which he already held.

Simpson made a cautious start as he assessed the obviously tough situation facing the company. He eventually decided that the Honda relationship was valuable, rather than, as he was seriously told by some of his senior colleagues, merely a means by which Honda took advantage of Rover for the sole purpose of making money. Then the policy of establishing Rover as an 'upmarket' manufacturer was emphasised and more attention was paid to improving operating performance.

In the product catalogue, the Rover 200/400 range was quickly a success, compared to its Rover-designed predecessors. Reservations about Rover's ability to develop and produce new engines were alleviated. The K series engine was highly competitive and achieved excellent quality levels. This was no accident: Rover had recruited experienced engineers to lead the team and had devoted considerable management effort to delivering a high-standard product. The stimulus of having direct comparisons with Honda's excellent engines no doubt acted as a spur. The K series installation in the Metro went ahead and was launched in 1990. The quality of the Metro improved substantially, but even then it was compromised in comparison with its European competition.

In 1989 Land Rover introduced the first Discovery. This was a new departure, aimed at a growing demand for family-oriented off-road leisure vehicles. The Discovery was an immediate success, giving Land Rover incremental volumes and market share.

Rover's position began to improve. As a result, 1989 and 1990 were years of steady progress towards higher operational standards and an improving financial position – published profits before interest were £73 million in 1989 and £65 million in 1990. (These figures should not be compared with earlier quoted figures because of accounting changes that took place when Rover Group became part of BAe.)

Following on from R8/YY the next joint project was the Rover 600. This model was a saloon car to fill the gap between the Rover 400 and Rover 800. The Rover 600 was closely derived from the Honda Accord, which Honda had decided to be the first car manufactured at Swindon. The Accord entered production at Swindon in 1992 and the Rover 600 at Cowley in 1993. At Land Rover, the second generation Range Rover was launched in 1994.

During this period, another management change followed when George Simpson was appointed a vice president of BAe, and John Towers replaced him as managing director of Rover.

Honda had been kept fully informed of the proceedings with British Aerospace and had no problems with continuing the relationship. Indeed, they agreed to a cross-shareholding between the two companies, which formalised the relationship to a greater extent than ever before.

Rover's operational performance continued to improve and indeed to accelerate as Towers accepted and implemented lessons from Honda. These facts and the fact that its car product range was, with the exceptions of the Mini and Metro, firmly based on Honda designs adapted to suit the Rover range, gave the company strength. Nevertheless, the financial position of its owner, British Aerospace, was revealed to be much weaker than had been seen at the time of the takeover. Indeed, had there been any true indication of BAe's financial prospects at the time of the takeover (as with DAF, a matter requiring remarkable foresight), it is doubtful whether it would have been right for Rover to have accepted the offer.

British Aerospace, although denying this in public, became anxious to sell Rover and to concentrate on its core businesses. In the late summer of 1993, it approached Honda to suggest that Honda might buy or at least take a bigger interest in Rover. Honda was strongly opposed to buying Rover outright for the simple - but in Honda's eyes overriding – reason that it believed that Rover should remain British. (Many people in Britain have had difficulty in believing this to be the main reason for Honda not buying Rover, but it is nevertheless true). What Honda did was to agree to raise its stake to 47.5 per cent with BAe retaining another 47.5 per cent and the last 5 per cent to be in some way held by Rover management and employees. Later, the BAe holding would be put on public offer.

By January 1994 Honda thought, because of what had gone on and what it had been told, that it had good reason to believe that it and BAe were very close to agreeing a deal on these terms. It was therefore with great surprise and consternation that Honda received the news that BAe intended to accept an offer from BMW to buy the whole of Rover for immediate cash unless Honda came up with at least as good a cash bid for the whole of Rover. Honda would not do this and Rover was sold to BMW.

Whether BMW knew the extent of Rover's product dependency on Honda is also doubtful – the agreements covering the various products were confidential. Presumably there was a general awareness and the attractions of the Rover four-wheel-drive business, known not to be dependent on Honda, made any risks to the car business worth taking.

The BMW Years 1994–2000

The Rover 400, launched in 1995, was a version of the Honda Civic, a mainstream medium car.

The Rover 200, launched in 1995, was developed from the 1989 Rover 200 and repositioned to compensate for the withdrawal of the Rover 100.

The Land Rover Freelander was launched in 1997 and opened up a new market for the brand.

Wholly engineered by Rover, the 75, launched in 1999, was the replacement for the Rover 600 and 800.

10

BMW: 1994–2000

On 31 January 1994, BMW took over the whole of Rover Group. At that time, this meant three assembly plants – Longbridge in Birmingham, Cowley in Oxford and Solihull, where Land Rovers were built – a body and pressings plant in Swindon and engine and transmission production at Longbridge. The company employed 33,600 people and produced eleven model ranges – six car lines under the Rover badge, the Mini and three off-road models under the Land Rover badge. The MG brand was about to be reintroduced.

BMW had never before tried to run a business it had not established in the first place, so this was an enormous meal to eat at one go. Why did they do it? Certainly within the BMW board there were some sceptics but the consensus was one of optimism that the takeover would give BMW far wider market coverage and access to under-exploited historic brands. The cynics said at the time, and since, that all they wanted was the brand value they recognised in the Mini and the Land Rover marques. Certainly the only positive outcome for them was ownership, in perpetuity, of the Mini brand.

The announcement of the takeover came as a shock to the employees of Rover Group and, it subsequently became clear, to those of BMW. Within Rover, the journey from the marques that had made up BL to the single Rover marque, known as 'Roverisation', had been a long-term struggle to become a BMW-like brand. BMW was constantly used as a shorthand for the image the company wanted. In that respect, the BMW takeover might have seemed like a dream come true. But like all major organisational change, it was destabilising for the people involved. In 1992, John Towers, the managing director, had introduced the New Deal, which offered security of employment in return for much more flexibility in working practices. At the same time, the organisation was restructured into business units, centred on the plants, where all of the functions worked together to achieve the best outcome for the model ranges or components for which they were responsible. This had fragmented the engineering organisation, in particular, and tended to focus loyalties at a plant level. The staff who had to deal with the new world of BMW had therefore just been through a major upheaval and were tending towards a Fortress Longbridge mentality.

BMW underestimated Rover's dependence on Honda. A complex series of technology and component-supply agreements were in place between Rover and Honda to support existing models, and much of the work on future models was dependent on Honda. At Cowley, the Rover 600 had just been launched, the same design, apart from the body panels, as the Honda Accord built at Swindon, and an engine installation programme to introduce a diesel was being developed.

At Longbridge, a restyle of the Rover 200 was underway. This three/five-door model was a restyled version of the previous Rover 200, shortened in an attempt to position the car slightly lower in the market to compensate for falling small-car sales. In parallel an all new Rover 400 was being worked on. This four/five-door model was a version of the Honda Civic, which Honda had decided to produce at Swindon. Both the 200 and 400 models were due for launch in 1995.

Other projects not related to Honda were also being worked on at Longbridge at the time of the takeover. During 1994 the Metro was face-lifted and rebadged Rover. This gave the model a small lift, but with no direct future replacement planned for the Mini or for the Rover 100, Rover seemed to be slowly exiting the small-car sector. Rover was, however, planning to re-enter the sports car sector. The MGF, a mid-engined, open two-seater using Rover 100 components, was also due for launch in 1995.

At Land Rover, there was almost no involvement with Honda, but a replacement for the Range Rover was approaching its launch date, as was a major Discovery update, and the Land Rover Freelander, eventually launched in 1998, was being discussed with potential overseas partners as investment to produce it at Solihull was not available.

The announcement of the BMW takeover had a paralysing effect on the Honda-related projects. Meetings and trips related to the Honda work were cancelled. Investment decisions about to be made were frozen. Despite having the contractual right to withdraw from all cooperation with Rover once it was owned by BMW, Honda chose not to do so. After a relatively short period the projects restarted but inevitably on a much less collaborative basis.

Rover Group had been working with Honda for fifteen years – much of a working lifetime. This, and maybe the underlying culture, had created a sort of diffidence that could also be interpreted as a lack of pride; it is certainly how BMW came to regard it. This diffidence, which is equally a willingness to learn, could have been a major opportunity for BMW to begin the process of sharing their best practice with an organisation that already had some knowledge on the way the Japanese did things. Had BMW both taught and listened, there was potential to create a joint enterprise that was a stronger and more efficient whole. But because of the assumption on the German side that imposing German management and working practices would be insulting, they kept the two companies apart. At an early meeting of senior management, Bernd Pischetsrieder (recently appointed chairman of the BMW management board, and the architect of the takeover) held up two bottles of different vintage wines. It was unthinkable, he said, that these should be mixed together. Like the wine, BMW and Rover were two strong and distinctive brands and they needed to be treated with the same respect. There was no immediate change to the management team. The company continued to be run by John Towers with engineering run by Nick Stephenson.

BMW is a company that has founded its success on excellence in engineering. It values and respects good engineers to the extent of having a reward structure that enables the most outstanding engineers to secure the benefits of senior management positions without having senior management responsibility. (This is in contrast to the situation at Rover, where gifted young engineers could be accelerated up the grade structure in recognition of their talents, when they did not have the management skills required and thus were less use than they had been at a lower level.) The BMW engineers, like the Rover engineers, were interested and excited by the takeover, or threatened by it, depending on which projects they were working on. At the time, the X5, BMW's first crossover four-wheel drive, was under development. There was a particular interest in what could be learnt from Land Rover and a fear that the project could be cancelled now the company owned a more appropriate brand for this type of product.

The Germans who dealt most with Rover Group spoke excellent English; meetings were held in English, even when they took place in Germany with a majority of senior German managers attending. There was no need,

BMW told Rover Group, to lay on language lessons for their employees – another example of keeping the unique culture of the new acquisition and avoiding the strengths of any of the key brands being diluted. As a result of the easy communication, there was a perception in Rover that BMW were 'people like us'. At the working level, dealing with Honda involved talking through interpreters and understanding different attitudes and cultural behaviour. Because language was no barrier, working with BMW, it seemed, was not like that.

Unfortunately, in other ways it was. Understanding the differences at the beginning might not have altered the outcome, but it could have made the experience more valuable for both partners. A cultural training programme subsequently introduced used the metaphor of a peach and a coconut to capture the key differences between the two national types that tended to cause problems and misunderstandings. The British presented themselves as soft and pleasant like a peach, but also like a peach at heart they were harder than they appeared to be and less caring. The Germans were coconuts: relatively hard and unforgiving on the surface, but with a much softer centre.

The Rover Group design director, Geoff Upex, put on an exhibition, which looked at the way in which German design differed from British design. It included photos of the interiors of ocean-going liners from the first half of the twentieth century. The British ships had all the cues that denoted luxury in the types and uses of materials and in the design of the furniture. The German version was recognisably functional and visually less appealing. In terms of comfort and fitness for purpose the German liner was very probably the better; as far as looking good was concerned, the British design won.

By the 1990s, the BMW engineers, designers and manufacturing teams had perfected the skills of making cars that were entirely functional and fit for purpose. Rover Group had made great strides in improving the fitness for purpose by adopting Honda approaches. There was more to do, however, and the company BMW took over was still relying too heavily on making the cars look good.

Products: Land Rover

At the time of the takeover Land Rover was producing the Defender, the Range Rover Classic and the Discovery. BMW had relatively little understanding of Land Rover. Because of the dynamic driving image of BMW products, the management was used to driving its products fast and in extreme conditions. The Land Rover engineers were frankly terrified when the same driving techniques were applied in a Defender, which is an unforgiving product if mishandled. However, the Land Rover design and management teams were intensely proud of their products and brand, and did have an understanding of what it was that made Land Rovers popular, and probably commanded more respect than the Rover teams as a result. The decision was taken, quite rightly, to carry on with both the X5 and the Land Rovers under development, and the off-road market sector has since proven to have room for both brands and a distinctive position for them both.

Senior-level visits took place, with outings arranged to Eastnor Castle. Land Rover products were tested on the slopes, forests, tracks and mud of the 5,000-acre estate.

The Defender was the hardest product for the Germans to understand. Early in their ownership their engineering director, Wolfgang Reitzle, sponsored an iconic, hugely appealing design exercise for a motor show. It was a open-topped, short-wheel-based yellow model with all the Land Rover styling cues enhanced. This would not have been feasible for production without a new platform. The Defender was and still is a chassis-based design without independent suspension or a monocoque body. All attempts to structure a programme for a new Defender foundered on the need to both retain its working credentials and to produce something that would sell in enough volume to justify the investment. It always made better business sense to use the technology from the other platforms to spin off lower-investment, higher-volume products.

The Range Rover was in the process of being replaced. After nearly a quarter of a century a whole new design was nearing completion, including a BMW diesel engine, which was a deal done before the takeover. This model, code-named P38A, was styled to be an evolution of the original, and this thinking, that bold changes should be avoided, had also led to the retention of the ladder chassis. It was launched after BMW took over. Despite being constrained by investment and engineering resource, the new Range Rover continued the brand's success, reinforcing its position as the most desirable premium 4x4. However, to BMW it was seen as a compromised design, not as good as the iconic Range Rover badge deserved. Later, when the 'hands off' approach had been abandoned, a team was set up in Munich to engineer a replacement. This was led by a

British engineer and was a mixed team, German and British. This ensured that the standards to which BMW was used to engineering vehicles were met, but the essence of what made a Range Rover unique was not lost. Ironically, BMW sold the company before the launch, but the approach was fully vindicated by the quality and success of the resulting product.

The Discovery was also approaching launch of its first major facelift, but here the compromises through lack of resource were even greater and the engineering integrity was not good. How to replace this product was not so clear. A design team led by a German engineer based at the Rover Group Engineering Centre in Gaydon had not made enough progress by the time the company was sold and the eventual replacement was engineered around Ford components.

The Freelander had been conceived at the beginning of the 1990s as a crossover product between Land Rover and Rover. The basic design was completed but shelved for lack of resource. It was subsequently resurrected as a better investment for Land Rover than an all-new Discovery, offering a lower price point and improved fuel consumption, as well as being at the beginning of a trend towards off-road/on-road vehicles. The Discovery replacement was downgraded to a facelift and the Freelander design went ahead. However, the investment in all-new manufacturing facilities had still been too big a morsel to swallow, and at the time that BMW took over, negotiations for a joint venture with overseas manufacture by a third party were well advanced. BMW cancelled this and went ahead with the investment at Solihull. The Freelander was finally launched in 1998 and took over from the Discovery as Europe's bestselling 4x4.

Products: Rover Cars

The treatment of Rover Cars lacked imagination, on all sides. The company was producing the Rover 200 and 400, Honda-based designs selling in the medium sector and perfectly good, competent products. They were replaced in 1995 by the heavily updated Rover 200 and the new Rover 400 based on Honda's next-generation Civic. These programmes were able to continue in production because of Honda's agreement to completing the engineering programme and ongoing parts supply.

The Rover and BMW managements decided that the next priority was the executive sector. The Rover 800 was in need of replacement, and so was the 600, which was a model where no further development would be supported by Honda. The decision was taken to replace both of them with one model – the Rover 75 – and this was largely the work of a British design team. Some of the pride that BMW expected Rover to feel in its heritage did find expression in this model, particularly in the interior design, and it might have become a classic if the brand had survived. The Rover 75 was undoubtedly the best engineered saloon car produced by Rover. The team was driven to prove that British engineers could match their German counterparts. On top of this, BMW provided a new level of engineering standards and test processes by which to prove the Rover 75 design.

The next new model priority was the Mini. From the outset BMW was convinced that there was a role for a 'new Mini' for both Rover and BMW and that it would be sold through both sales networks.

What happened to the Mini highlights the differences in the approaches and attitudes of the two companies. The BMW design team, led by Reitzle, was very keen to take this iconic brand and image and bring it up to date. They believed they understood what 'Mini-ness' was. The Rover team were equally keen, given the investment was available, and were certain they understood the Mini, and its history. Each organisation was allowed to set up a design team and bring a proposal to a senior-level meeting, with the successful proposal being allowed to go forward as a project. The results showed how different were the two sides' perceptions of the Mini.

The Rover team felt that the Mini represented innovative engineering, compact size and brilliant packaging. Their proposal had a rear-mounted engine, allowing a much shorter, more space-efficient package. Their body style was quirky and in the modern idiom, as the original Mini had been.

The BMW version was a conventionally engineered small-sector car, with a body style that captured the spirit of the original Mini. They looked at the car and saw an icon, and they reproduced it, taking into account the expectations of the modern customer for performance and accommodation. The Rover team was outraged when this design won, even though the team to deliver it was set up in the UK and was largely staffed with British engineers. Hindsight tells us that BMW was right. There was no need to be extreme, in engineering terms, as the original had been. The market was there for a small car that was a recreation of a style icon without engineering innovation.

The final priority for Rover Cars was a mid-sized car in the medium sector to replace the Rover 200 and 400. To avoid direct competition with the BMW 3 Series, a very distinctive product was needed, and BMW might have expected the Rover engineers and designers to know what a truly great Rover car would look like. But so many years spent trying to avoid major investment and to make best use of whatever Honda had to offer had made it difficult for anyone to imagine what that might be. A team was formed to work on the replacement, but there was not the urgency put into this as into the replacement of, for example, the Range Rover, where BMW and Rover had a clear understanding of what excellence could be.

BMW had also come to the conclusion that it needed a car to compete in the sector below the 3 Series, and there was undoubtedly impatience with the failure to realise an acceptable design for a Rover in this sector, when a BMW team could, and did with the 1 Series, make a good and eminently marketable product.

One major factor in the slow progress of Rover's medium car was that doubts about the future of Rover were becoming prevalent in BMW. A medium car would require a large investment, which seemed untenable given the desperate state of Rover's finances. At the point when BMW decided to pull the plug on Rover the new medium car was still on the shelf.

Products: Power Train

While at least initially there was a reticence to bring the vehicle engineering teams together, from day one power train engineering was integrated. The first step was to benchmark the engines that were in production. Fortunately for Rover, the most recently introduced engine, the K series, was competitive in terms of performance, quality and cost. Benchmarking this engine gave the BMW engineers confidence in Rover. This was particularly important as for BMW the engine is always the heart of any car.

Almost immediately a joint team was set up to design an all new 2-litre, four-cylinder petrol engine. The best Rover engine engineers were drafted to Munich to evolve the concept with their BMW counterparts. It was a complex task because of the wide range of vehicle requirements. For example, BMW vehicles were rear-wheel drive and Rovers were front-wheel drive. The resultant engine was more compact and cost-effective than BMW would normally design and higher performing and more fuel efficient than Rover would design.

After two years of designing the new engine the critical decision on where it should be manufactured had to be made. There were three possibilities: the existing engine plants in Munich and Graz in Austria, or a completely new greenfield site in the UK. After several months of intensive study and very thorough analysis to ensure that all information was compatible and fair, BMW management made the decision. Somewhat to the surprise of Rover management, Hams Hall near Birmingham was selected and immediately a project team of production engineers under Rover leadership was set up to deliver the project.

Throughout the period of BMW ownership there was a progressive integration of the power train engineering teams. Rover engineers worked in Munich and BMW engineers worked in the UK. The senior transmission engineer for all BMW and Rover products was appointed from the Rover team and at one stage the UK engineering team was led by a BMW director. The work on joint projects and the integration of the teams resulted in a better working relationship than in other parts of the engineering organisation. The Rover power train engineers often felt resentment being the butt of 'collaborator' jokes.

The Beginning of the End

There was a fundamental difference in the way in which each company regarded target-setting. The BMW way was to under-promise and over-deliver. The Rover way was to set targets that were unlikely ever to be met, on the basis that setting your sights high is more likely to lead to over-performance. BMW could not understand how Rover consistently failed to hit their targets, and this led to a difficult working relationship between the senior teams.

The two most powerful men in BMW were Pischetsrieder and Reitzle. The first had been the power behind the takeover, and was optimistic about the results; the latter, who was behind the BMW designs of the time and had a clear vision of what represented good design, was against it. In 1995, as Pischetsrieder's optimism was not matched by performance, Reitzle replaced him as Rover chairman and began to make regular trips to the UK to review and consult on progress, or the lack of it. In truth these visits probably did more harm than good, further convincing the management that their autonomy was not real. Finally, in 1996, John Towers resigned and Dr Walter Hasselkus was sent over from BMW to take over as CEO. He had run the UK operation for BMW, and turned round the problem motorcycle division, so was an obvious choice, and was largely welcomed by the senior management.

The company kept on losing significant sums of money. This was due to a number of factors, including the strength of the pound and the poor reception of the revamped mid-range models. It was also because BMW spent money when Rover Group, in its self-managed days, would have made do and mended. BMW undoubtedly thought it was still not spending enough. The state of, for example, the Solihull factory where Land Rovers were made was in its eyes a disgrace. Reitzle, for whom appearances mattered, said in one senior management conference that it was unthinkable to leave things as they were, but equally unthinkable to reach in a single leap the standard that BMW would set. The gap was too big.

As the task of turning Rover round became manifestly problematic, the Rover 75 was launched, and Pischetsrieder took the opportunity to put pressure on the UK government to support it with grants. This did not help the early sales of the Rover 75 and had the effect of reducing consumer confidence in the brand.

Hasselkus resigned in 1998 and was replaced by Walter Sämann, who had none of the Anglophile credentials of Hasselkus and was effectively a German figurehead overseeing what had become a company run from Munich. The now rapid demand for Rover staff to begin to behave like German employees was a source of tension. Language classes were at last introduced, but an hour a week for engineers who had studied no foreign language since the age of 16 was never going to enable them to participate in meetings, which suddenly began to be held in German. This was an obvious problem. Less obvious was the enormous cultural gap between the way in which the German management behaved and the way in which the British management behaved. Alarmed at the loss of engineering resource (ironically mostly being taken on by Jaguar, soon to be joined back together with Land Rover), an HR consultant was sent over from Munich to find out why. Why, when in Germany it was the pinnacle of an engineer's ambition to be taken on by BMW, did engineers in the UK not want to work for them?

This exercise established that a UK engineer would expect his manager to be supportive, to coach him through the tasks, to discuss solutions to problems with him. The German managers, they complained, just told them what to do. They saw this as diminishing them, as if they were simply a cog in a machine. A German engineer, on the other hand, expected his manager to respect his engineering skills and simply to tell him what part of the overall process it was his job to carry out. The German employees would always understand their position in a team or department; administrative assistants, when introduced to visitors, would explain what it was the job of the department to achieve, and the way in which they contributed to that. When this difference was pointed out to the German chief engineer on one of the major projects being run in the UK, he was aghast. He could never behave as if his staff did not know what they were doing without his help, he said. It would be insulting.

By 1999, it was obvious that BMW was at risk from the continued losses at Rover Group. It was equally clear that there were no easy solutions.

The End

The continuing crisis at Rover Group was having a negative impact on BMW, and the Management Board, particularly the Quandt family who were still the majority shareholders, found the situation intolerable. Pischetsrieder and, to everyone's surprise, Reitzle, resigned from the board of BMW in 1999. By this time, some of the key British managers left in Rover Group had been invited into the elite OFK group, the top tier of BMW management grades. Even so, none of them had positions from which they could influence the final outcome; Germans filled all of the key positions and the British management had been marginalised. This, unlike the beginning of the relationship when the involvement of German management would have been valuable and would have compensated for weaknesses in the British team, was the wrong time to ignore the Rover Group staff. They had experience of managing crisis and failure; BMW did not.

During the last few months, the tensions mounted within Rover Group. Friendships had been formed between the two organisations and passion for the products, particularly Land Rover, had begun to grow in the German cohort working alongside the British. It was hard for those resident in Britain, working on Rover Group projects. The feeling of failing was new to them, and it created more tension and distress as a result of its unfamiliarity.

On 14 March 2000, the Munich-based newspaper *Suddeutsche Zeitung* reported that Rover Group was about to be sold to a venture capital company. The senior German management working in the UK returned to Munich and were unavailable, in meetings. On Thursday 16 March, the senior management tier in Rover – Germans and British – were told to attend a briefing session at 12 p.m. The senior team arrived at 12.15 and announced they could announce nothing until 1 p.m. By 1 p.m. the timing had changed to 1.30 p.m. Finally, the senior German Director in each location went through a set of carefully prepared slides announcing the sale of Rover Group to Alchemy Partners. These slides presented this decision as a logical and inevitable step, which had been forced upon BMW by circumstances outside its control – the value of the pound, uncertainty about UK government grant support and falling sales of Rover products since 1995.

There was no slide for the sale of Land Rover to Ford, just an announcement that this had been agreed. It was apparent that the delay in announcing the Rover Cars information had been caused by a protracted decision-making process around Land Rover. The value of the brand was well recognised by BMW, but it had its own four-wheel-drive vehicle and another under development. And the sale allowed them to recoup at least some of the millions it had cost them to buy and own Rover Group. So at the final hour, the sale went ahead.

The Aftermath

Alchemy Partners' plan for Rover Cars was that the operation would be scaled down to the production of the Rover 75 and sports cars. BMW was providing capital that would pay for the required redundancy and allow an investment in a continued, smaller operation. Brokered by the unions, an alternative bid to keep the company going at the same scale was put forward by John Towers, Nick Stephenson and two local businessmen – the 'gang of four' as they came to be known. Alchemy withdrew, as this offer apparently avoided the need for redundancies, and the company, with ownership of the MG marque and a right to use the Rover marque, with all of the facilities at Longbridge, was transferred into the ownership of Phoenix, as the consortium was known. The Mini brand was retained by BMW.

Land Rover, after due diligence was complete, transferred to Ford.

The division of the staff was painful and protracted. The manufacturing workforces at Longbridge and Solihull were transferred to Phoenix and Ford respectively; the Cowley workforce was retained by BMW. At a staff level it was not so straightforward. Anyone obviously working on a Land Rover or Rover Cars project had the right to a transfer of employment to the new owner. Similarly, anyone working on a Mini had a right to remain with BMW. The two new owners had first to create organisation charts to define what jobs were available and what needed to be filled; BMW had to work out how to proceed with the development of the Mini. In some ways, this last was the easy part. By this time the ill-feeling towards BMW was extreme, and the contempt of BMW management for much of the engineering effort of Rover Group was equally strong, so the Mini project team members applied for jobs in Land Rover and were thankfully released by BMW.

Ford wanted Land Rover to grow – they had just completed an expansion at Jaguar taking it into new sectors (with disastrous financial consequences as it turned out, but this was not yet apparent) so they were prepared to sponsor a substantial infrastructure at Land Rover and the number of people automatically following the projects was not enough. Almost anyone who was able to avoid a transfer to Phoenix applied for a job in Land Rover. It was a heartbreaking task for the embryonic Land Rover management to make a selection, knowing that those who remained with Phoenix could expect far less job security than those who signed up with Ford. It was particularly hard for those fairly close to retirement. Within five years, an individual then aged 55 who had stayed with Land Rover would be sure of a well-supported retirement; an ex-Phoenix employee would be facing another five years of working and a much reduced pension at the end.

The separation of Land Rover from BMW was managed in an orderly fashion, with both Ford and BMW working to ensure that neither company was disadvantaged. BMW continued to support the development of the new Range Rover; Ford went ahead with pressing the panels for the new Mini at Solihull.

As a footnote, it is worth comparing the Cowley plant in Oxford today, as a BMW plant, with the one it took over in 1994. It is transformed. Redundant buildings have been demolished. All remaining buildings have been refurbished to look neat and functional. The uniforms of the workers are good quality and universally worn, unlike the tired, grey workwear that was anything but uniform in Rover Cars. The entrance to the plant, the car parking, the security, the traffic flow have all been improved. Rover Cars did not spend money on such things – there was no money to spend that did not directly translate into new vehicles. But there is a link between a tidy plant and a quality brand.

MG Rover – BMW – Ford, 2000–07

The City Rover was a small car based on the Tata Indicar. It was added to the MG Rover product range in 2003.

The third-generation Range Rover, launched in 2002, was designed by BMW and produced at Solihull under Ford ownership. (HMC)

The Discovery 3, launched in 2004, was all new and wholly engineered by Land Rover with Ford engines. (Jaguar Land Rover)

The Range Rover Sport, launched in 2005, was a new sporty model derived from the Discovery. (HMC)

The Freelander 2, launched in 2007, was engineered from a Ford global platform with Ford and Peugeot engines. (Jaguar Land Rover)

11

The Final Chapter – MG Rover: 2000–05

BMW wanted to divest itself of the liability for Rover Cars and the Longbridge facility. To this end, it arranged a deal with Alchemy, a venture capital organisation, which had concluded that a niche sports car business was viable, based at Longbridge and perpetuating the MG brand. This deal would have resulted in large-scale redundancies, at BMW's cost, and would have left the liability for the pension rights accrued by all those workers losing their jobs with BMW.

It is hard to say whether the outcome of the Alchemy deal, if it had gone through, would have been a business with long-term potential. It was trumped by an alternative offer from a consortium of ex-Rover directors and businessmen. This offer kept the Longbridge factory open, building the same range of cars, including the newly launched Rover 75. Once this offer was on the table it was almost inevitable it would be accepted because it apparently avoided the need for massive redundancies and kept the Longbridge factory intact. This was clearly a much better outcome in terms of short-term public relations and there was jubilation among the workforce and from local politicians. The Phoenix consortium took over all the liabilities, including the pension scheme, and BMW provided the cash, which it would have cost them to close down the bulk of the business, to allow it to continue to operate.

The 'gang of four' behind the Phoenix consortium were: John Towers, who had previously run Rover and who had a manufacturing background; Nick Stephenson, an engineer with a long history within Rover Group, and a car enthusiast; John Edwards, a car dealer with a Rover franchise; Peter Beale, a partner in an accountancy firm.

MG Rover was launched with a fanfare of positive publicity. It inherited a product range consisting of the Rover 200, 400 and 75 models and the MGF. The engineering team embarked on a busy programme of facelifts and upgrades. The medium car project was resurrected, but there was no prospect of generating the cash to invest in it. The Rover 200 and 400 were tweaked and renamed 25 and 45. An estate car version of the 75 was added. High-performance MG versions of all saloons were developed. With little prospect of commercial justification, the MGF suspension was completely redesigned, a rear-wheel-drive, V8-engined version of the 75 and, most strangely of all, a super car based on the Qvale Mangusta was added to the range. Despite this activity, sales fell year on year. In an attempt to halt the decline, the company sought to find a new small car to sell through its network. No company with significant European sales was prepared to supply a product, but the Indian company Tata was keen to offer the Indicar. The resultant cooperation produced the City Rover. Unfortunately at that time Indian auto industry standards were well below European standards and the City Rover was not successful. MG Rover sales continued to fall from 198,000 in 2000 to 135,000 in 2003.

Without a partner capable of funding a recovery, it was impossible for the operation to survive: the board may honestly have believed that a partnership was possible, but it is hard to see why anyone would have been sanguine about this. Any prospective partner would have seen that the company had potential liabilities far greater than its assets. The prospect of running a car company is an exciting one; designing and developing cars is exciting and the company had some fun doing this, with ever more extreme versions of the ageing models and the takeover of a sports car company. It is also possible that they felt they could make a success of it and reap the rewards.

The risks for the architects of the takeover were business risks, with little personal financial risk. The National Audit Office report noted that as a result of the way the company was structured, 'profitable elements of the business were separate from MG Rover Group Limited, the company which manufactured cars and employed the majority of the group's workforce.' A subsequent report was commissioned from BDO Stoy Hayward, which revealed that five executives (the 'Gang of Four' and chief executive Kevin Howe) took £42m in pay and pensions from the troubled firm as it collapsed.

The four were banned from holding company directorships for varying periods of time up to six years, but no criminal prosecutions were brought. They were criticised for the apparent misuse of funds as described above, for failing to support the enquiry with full and honest information and, in one case, for deleting information and offloading costs onto MG Rover as the enquiry commenced. Mention was also made of excessive payments to a Chinese 'consultant', who was paid £1.69m for fifteen months' work. There was undoubtedly damage to their reputations. The main casualties, however, were the 6,300 workers whose jobs were lost when the company collapsed in 2005, owing its creditors £1.3bn and unable to meet its pension liabilities.

If jobs are judged to be the most important thing, the deal did offer employment to more people than Alchemy would have done, for five years. All the employees were then left without the redundancy payments and retirement benefits they could have expected from a long career with the same company – and most of the employees would have had long careers – and which they would have received if BMW had been allowed to sell to Alchemy. Whether Alchemy would have managed a secure future for fewer people for more than five years is a matter for speculation, although the subsequent success of other residual niche British brands would suggest it might. But even if it had also failed, the bulk of the workforce would have had their accrued benefits protected.

The Longbridge plant was a derelict printing works when Herbert Austin took it over in 1905. Located on a hill on the edge of town and the country, it was not a sensible place to build cars. Today, any company lucky enough to be able to afford a greenfield site would look for flat ground with good accessibility (as with Hams Hall built by BMW). However, cars had been built there for 100 years; generations from the same families had worked there; it had once been an industrial city producing everything from castings to completed vehicles. In the 1970s it was the view, from inside and possibly from the public as well, that it was too big to fail. During the next twenty-five years there were times (after the industrial relations were sorted out, during the relationship with Honda) when there was a prospect of continuous improvement and profitability. By the time it did fail, there was nothing left worth saving except jobs and the emotional heritage.

12

The Causes of the Failure of BLMC in Sequence

This book has told the story of the thirty-seven-year life of the car business of the British Leyland Motor Corporation (BLMC) from 1968 until 2005, when the remnant of that car business (MG Rover) failed. The story has been one of disastrous failure in the first seven years, followed by thirty years during which various owners and managements tried to make a commercially enduring company from what remained. Nobody succeeded.

Not quite all was failure. Although no enduring company emerged, two marques (Jaguar and Land Rover) now flourish in Indian ownership and BMW produces the Mini at Cowley. Unipart, the BLMC parts supply company, is still in business, although largely in non-automotive parts. The collaboration with Honda was mainly successful. Most of all, the success of Michael Edwardes, helped by the good sense of the workforce (but not their trade unions), in curing the company's industrial relations sickness has been of national importance.

The causes of failure will be considered in three phases:

1. 1968–77: The Failure of the Grand Design
2. 1977–84: The Failure of a Modest Ambition
3. 1984–2005: The Failure to Endure Commercial Reality

Part 1. 1968–77: The Failure of the Grand Design

Throughout this phase, the original aim – to establish a large, world-competitive company – applied, although there were two owners. From

1968 until the failure in 1975 it was owned by the shareholders while the two years from 1975 until 1977 were the first two years of government ownership during which the original aim (if unrealistically) was retained.

The key to achieving the aim was that the company's weak profitability should not weaken further until rationalisation brought its confidently expected benefits of increased profit from a rationalised vehicle range bringing operating cost savings and, in the longer term, investment savings. For the five years until 1973, profits held up well, linked to consistently high car production, helped by the introduction of the Marina in 1971, even though that model increased complexity, and by an increase in the UK market in 1971, 1972 and 1973. Ominously, however, the UK market share had fallen steadily from 41 per cent in 1968 to 32 per cent in 1973, reflecting increasing competitive pressure. Then in 1974 sales declined, and with that decline production fell from 876,000 to 738,000, followed by another fall to 605,000 in 1975. Accompanying these falls was a catastrophic drop in profits to barely above break-even in 1974 and a loss of £75 million in 1975. BLMC was in no condition to stand the losses and the government was called in during 1975.

The reason for the fall in production is clear. The vehicle range with which BLMC had started was getting older and losing competitiveness and some models were dropped without replacement. More importantly, the new vehicles such as the Maxi and especially the Allegro replacing the 1100/1300 in 1974, far from being the 'better' vehicles so confidently predicted, were vastly inferior and achieved much lower sales.

The position was made worse by the fact that strikes went on unabated and yet no serious attempt was made to tackle the industrial relations problem, which lost the company sales directly because of the stoppages and indirectly because of the company's deteriorating reputation.

The lack of action on industrial relations also perpetuated the inability to improve manufacturing efficiency. So manufacturing costs remained uncompetitive and sales fell because improvements in vehicle quality and reliability could not be introduced. Moreover, the cost savings that had been confidently forecast to come from rationalisation did not materialise. This was due to management inaction – if a model was dropped, related activities were allowed to continue. What was more unforgivable was that even with the drop in production, no attempt was made to reduce production capacity. The infrastructure that had existed to support car production of over one million cars remained as large as ever with car production reduced by more than one quarter.

The downward path was lengthened for a further two years from 1975 by the Ryder team's unrealistically optimistic view of the company's future and lack of perception of the real reasons for failure. These factors led them to recommend government ownership with the same ambitious aims that BLMC had had and, especially damaging, very much the same operational management. It was during this period that the company's great hope, the SD1, was introduced (1976). The car got a good reception, but it soon became clear that its quality was so low and reliability faults so many that potential customers turned away and that another new model would be a failure.

Nevertheless, in 1976 production and profits increased – the latter helped by favourable currency fluctuations – but results deteriorated in 1977, with profits barely above break-even. The National Enterprise Board lost what little remaining faith it had in the company's board and senior management and strongly represented to the government that both had to be changed. The government accepted this view.

Who or what was responsible for the failure? This raises the question of whether BLMC should have been formed. With the benefit of hindsight, the conclusion is probably 'no'. It is certainly possible that some form of amalgamation of the vehicle businesses would have happened because of commercial pressures, without government involvement. Whether, given the inherent weaknesses of the car companies involved and the sheer difficulty of moving from where they were to commercial success, such a commercially-driven move would have been more successful, is very doubtful. What is more certain is that in the actual circumstances the Ryder team should have recommended closure or, at the very least, a far less ambitious and more realistic plan and many more changes to the management.

Turning to the direct causes of failure, for the loss of car sales the primary responsibility lay with the top product engineering management for the poor products that were introduced. For the general inaction on industrial relations and the failure to realise any benefits from rationalisation the responsibility lay with the top management.

Not only was this stage a disaster in itself, showing up all the weaknesses inherent in BLMC, but it left the company in so weak a state that recovery to a sustainable commercial state was, at best, a very doubtful possibility.

Part 2. 1977–84: The Failure of a Modest Ambition

This part covers the period from 1977, when Michael Edwardes became chairman and chief executive with the remit to transform the company to one with a sustainable future and one capable of being taken out of government ownership, until 1984 when this aim was abandoned as a priority and privatisation took its place.

To have any chance of achieving the aim, Edwardes realised that three things had to be done: the company size had to be reduced to match its sales volumes, thus reducing excess costs; the industrial relations situation had to be transformed; and the product development capability had to be vastly improved to make the product range competitive.

He found things to be even worse than expected. The previous management sales forecasts were clearly much too optimistic and had to be lowered, which would reduce profits. There was a gap of about four years until the much-needed new medium car could be introduced. To add to that problem, the new small car (Metro) that had been given ill-considered priority had been shown by a styling clinic to be so poorly styled that Edwardes took the decision to accept the extra delays that would result and have it re-styled. To add to the volume worries, the SD1 quality and reliability deficiencies were starting to show up. Not surprisingly, total car sales volumes continued to fall from 611,000 in 1978 to 504,000 in 1979 and to 395,000 in 1980.

However, under Edwardes's leadership one of the major problems, industrial relations, was solved, but this took until 1981 and, as he left in 1982, he was unable to develop the benefits that this made possible.

Doing something about product development was equally difficult. It was clear that internal resources were completely inadequate to fill the gap in new model introductions with which he was faced or to develop a competitive full range of vehicles. With volumes already falling, the only solution was to find a partner and, after a long search, in 1979 this was found in the Honda Motor Company. Again, the benefits inevitably took time to come through and the first model from the partnership came into production in 1981, just preceded by BL's own small car, the re-styled Metro. By this time too, BL's new medium cars, the Maestro and Montego, were under development, although the first of the pair, the Maestro, would not be introduced until 1983. When they did come into production they, like the Metro, showed an improvement over their in-house predecessors such as the Allegro and SD1 but were not the outstanding cars that the company needed for recovery.

On the remaining major weakness, manufacturing efficiency, Edwardes had made improvement practicable by removing the industrial relations barrier to improvements, but there was then little time left in his tenure. He did, however, close the Triumph factory at Liverpool in 1978 and Abingdon MG in 1980, which started to match capacity to sales and so reduce costs. The link with Honda also provided the opportunity for learning from one of the most efficient production companies in the world, but this was for the future.

The Edwardes era was one of achievement, which, in addition to the practical benefits, gave a fillip to the morale of the company. However, the fall in volumes of the first three years meant that more government funding than had been forecast would be needed and the company fell into a period of serious losses that continued until after he left in 1982. Thus the aim of attaining commercial viability was not achieved, but what had been achieved was a strong platform for further progress that gave a genuine hope of eventual success.

Progress continued in two fields after Edwardes's departure. The freedom from industrial relations problems was built upon and thereafter was neither an obstacle to improving performance nor a hindrance to sales. The relationship with Honda on products was extended and strengthened. However, the doubts and even antagonism towards Honda, which existed with some of the senior executives in finance, manufacture, purchase, and quality and reliability, prevented advantage being taken of the Honda expertise in the operational areas for which they were responsible.

Although the first two years after Edwardes demonstrated that the industrial relations problems existed no longer, the Honda relationship was strengthened and BL's own development capability seemed to be improving, the government decided that the possibility of independence from government funding was too far away and that it would not wait for recovery before selling BLMC. Thus the aim for the company became to privatise. Another era had started.

Part 3. The Failure to Endure Commercial Reality: 1984-2005

For the first two years of this period, the company continued with the same organisation and management that had existed since Edwardes left in 1982, but now a great deal of senior management time was taken up with privatisation issues.

The first unit to go was Jaguar, sold by being floated on the stock exchange in 1984. Then, in early 1985, talks began with General Motors for the sale of the commercial vehicle business, which included Land Rover. These talks eventually failed because the British government changed its mind at the very last minute after all the terms had been agreed and government approval given, and withdrew its approval because of political fears of selling Land Rover to a non-British company. Overlapping with the GM bid, Ford had made an approach for the car business, but the government withdrawal brought this to an end as well.

In 1986 Graham Day took over as chairman and chief executive, bringing to an end the split role. The importance of privatisation over all else was also emphasised by his remit. He succeeded. A deal was completed in February 1987 with DAF for DAF and the BL commercial vehicle operations to form a joint company. Cars and Land Rover were sold to British Aerospace in March 1988. Other independent units such as Unipart were disposed of by management buyout or commercial sale.

While all this was going on the company received two major setbacks, or at least serious warnings that in spite of some progress serious deficiencies still existed in its product development and product quality standards. The first of these was the very poor quality of the Rover Sterling/800 range – a joint development with Honda (whose version topped the US charts for customer satisfaction while the Rover US version was near the bottom) and the second the deficiencies of the Honda Ballade produced by Rover for Honda at Longbridge.

This stage, the start of the privatisation era, took BLMC out of government ownership and was therefore a success for the privatisation policy, but it left the company with still much to do to attain competitive operational standards.

After the takeover of the Cars Group and of Land Rover, the aim for Rover became once again that of attaining commercial viability and progress was made. Product standards had improved and at last the operating executives were told to listen to and learn from Honda. This meant that use was made of Honda's advice on improving manufacturing efficiency and product quality and reliability. The view of the president of Honda Europe, an immensely able executive with a lifetime's experience in manufacturing, was that with three more years of improvement, the company would have become world competitive.

Unfortunately, it was not to be given those three years. British Aerospace's own financial position turned out to be much weaker than had been thought at the time of the Rover sale and it became necessary to sell Rover to strengthen the parent company. In 1994 Rover was sold to BMW.

To many people in Rover, BMW appeared to be a good owner for Rover – a technically strong company able to take the improvements started in British Aerospace further, even though the links with Honda were lost. However, BMW did not manage to make the difference they might have hoped to, and Rover continued to lose money. The point came when BMW, or at least its owners, would no longer support those losses. Land Rover was sold to Ford and the core of the company was 'sold' on very generous terms to a consortium of four executives who planned to run the company (MG Rover) as an independent business. The settlement kept alive a remnant of BLMC, but the prospects for MG Rover as an independent company could not be considered promising.

It is not clear why the four executives who took on the ownership of MG/Rover did so. They were experienced motor industry men, and although BMW provided a generous dowry it must have been clear to them that the chances of a tiny independent company surviving were very low.

13

The Causes of Failure – The Underlying Weaknesses

This chapter will cover underlying problems that existed in BLMC, either for the whole of its existence or for significant periods. Overwhelmingly, the most important weakness was in engineering, both in product engineering and in manufacturing engineering. Management was a weakness, especially in the first few years, but the management at that time had been handed a near-impossible task because of very optimistic assessments of what the newly formed company could do. The importance of engineering, the effects of government ownership and its inconsistent policies regarding the company and another underlying problem – over-optimistic forecasting – are discussed below.

Engineering

All companies rely on the success of their products – essentially how successful they are in satisfying the customers in terms of performance, looks, price, running costs and, most of all, reliability and freedom from faults – to generate a level of profit at least sufficient to sustain itself.

Many inputs go to decide the basic design of the vehicle – for example, the target customer, available technology, the investment required, its place in the range of vehicles being produced by the company, forecasts of production costs, sales prices, sales volumes and levels of profitability. The higher the quality of those inputs, the greater is likely to be the success of the product.

However, the importance of these inputs pales into if not insignificance then something approaching it, compared with the dependence on product engineering for the design and manufacturing engineering for efficient production, which is also, to a significant extent, dependent on good design.

Thus the functions that need to dominate in a vehicle company to ensure that the product is 'right' are product and manufacturing engineering. The fact that this was never so in the Cars Group of BLMC was an underlying and lasting weakness, and trying to put this right was a major difficulty that was never realised.

Further, because of the importance of the engineering at the operating level it is vital that the most senior management levels be imbued with the belief that engineering excellence should dominate the company. This was far from the case in BLMC, whose senior ranks always lacked sufficient numbers of experienced and knowledgeable engineers.

It is in these senior ranks that decisions that affect the future of a company are made. It is very important that there is an adequate engineering influence put into these decisions. The contrast between BLMC and, say, Honda and BMW, was marked. In Honda, for example, the president (chief executive) had almost always, since the retirement of Soichiro Honda, been the head of Honda research and development (the product-development department). In the other top posts there were many engineers, either from manufacturing or product development.

Of course, those filling senior posts need qualities in addition to engineering qualifications and experience – general intelligence, awareness and judgment of society's needs, a drive to get things done. The whole organisation, too, must have functions such as finance, sales and marketing, market research, personnel and so on, but these functions should be there to provide support for the engineering functions, and not, as is too often the case, to be the lead function: finance, for instance, was too often allowed to behave this way.

Indeed, in both BMW and Honda the company ethos was that engineering had to be of the highest possible standard. BLMC did not develop anything that could be called an 'ethos' or defining characteristic, and certainly not an engineering one.

On a personal note from one of the authors: supporting the case for engineers at all levels, it is Carver's belief that if he, instead of being something of a Jack of all trades, had been a qualified and experienced engineer, he would have been more confident about the recommendations and decisions that he made in his planning role in BL. He also believes that had he had an engineering background, he would have had more influence with the engineering ranks in the company and have been more successful in persuading them to listen to Honda.

Of course, engineering excellence requires a disciplined, practical approach. From the late 1950s, Ford had imported from its parent the process for developing new cars. This process depended heavily on consumer research and targeting specific customers. In the 1960s, Issigonis was an autocratic leader and to him the Ford process was anathema. The engineers' role was to create products, which customers would appreciate for their functional benefits. Styling was a necessary but subordinate evil. Issigonis's approach had been highly successful for the Mini and the 1100 but had failed for the 1800 and Maxi. Although Issigonis's influence waned in BLMC, the attitudes continued to prevail in the engineering teams. Consumer targeting did become part of BLMC's product development process, but with varying degrees of success.

During the development of new models, prototype components and vehicles are assembled to prove out the new designs. The prototypes are hand-built and very expensive. In the cash-constrained environment that prevailed in BLMC it was tempting to limit the number of prototypes. Testing was limited to driving on public roads and airfields. The UK was a particularly benign place to test cars. Roads were good and did not have the pavé found on the Continent. Continuous high-speed running was not possible as it was in Germany. Weather did not have extreme temperatures. Additionally, the cars that entered volume manufacture were significantly different from the hand-built prototypes that had been tested. In these circumstances it was almost inevitable that the first customers found faults that had been missed in development.

Ford and Vauxhall had seen the benefit of building their own dedicated test sites at Lommel in Belgium and Millbrook in the UK respectively. These sites were fully operational by the mid 1960s. It was not until 1976 that BLMC would have its own test site at Gaydon, and it took a further fifteen years to install a full suite of modern test facilities. Up until then, BLMC used the publicly owned MIRA test site. This was available to all manufacturers, was expensive to hire and had security constraints. The problem for BLMC was that investment in engineering test facilities had no immediate payback even though it is clear, certainly to experienced vehicle engineers, that failure to test properly on proper facilities leads to quality problems, which are the things that customers dislike most and which are one, perhaps the greatest, reason for losing sales. This lack of timely investment in adequate test facilities came directly from the lack of engineering experience in BLMC's higher ranks.

But it is not only that. Field failures should be understood and then future designs should take the solutions into account and the test programme should be changed to replicate the conditions under which the field failures occurred. This 'closed loop' process was sadly lacking. New model after new model suffered recurring faults.

From the mid 1980s onwards the product development process improved as new test facilities came on stream and Rover engineers worked alongside Honda. Development on joint models enforced a disciplined commitment to robust prototype phases, with the learning from each phase being built into the next. A culture of holding events where everyone, including the suppliers, analysed the findings from the testing and jointly agreed the modifications was introduced. Drawings were updated and the engineers, suppliers and manufacturing engineers could all be sure they were working on the latest design. This process also improved the speed of product development, as the timing of the end of the phase was a commitment that could not be moved.

A further improvement in engineering performance occurred when BMW's new model process and test standards were adopted. As a result, the last car wholly designed and engineered by Rover, the Rover 75, was undoubtedly the best car ever produced by the company.

Government Involvement and Vacillation

It may seem a strange thing to see government involvement as an underlying weakness, but it was nonetheless a factor in the lack of success of BLMC until the company went into the ownership of British Aerospace in 1988.

In the first place, the company was put together with government encouragement and some, if small, financial assistance. The companies involved wanted a merger but, left to themselves, a less ambitious entity would have emerged and this entity would have taken better account of the underlying weaknesses of the constituent companies. In the end, from 1988, without government involvement, commercial reality did take over – the untenable parts were closed down and after various rather tortuous moves, a successful car company made up of Jaguar and Land Rover emerged, small compared with the original BLMC car group but, as the last chapter in this book describes, strong, successful and growing. Other parts of the original group, too, still survive and, with involvement from China, the Longbridge factory, which was closed with so much unhappiness in 2005, is reviving.

In contrast, BLMC in 1968 was, encouraged by government involvement, an unrealistically over-ambitious company. Not surprisingly, BLMC's underlying weaknesses proved too much for its management. When it failed in 1975 the government went further and took over the company. By this time the company was much reduced in size, with fundamental problems not resolved, but the government accepted the recommendation of its advising team that, with little change, a successful company would emerge.

Much the same operational management was allowed to continue and, inevitably, the failure continued. At last the government, advised by its creation, the National Enterprise Board, acted quickly and decisively to try to halt the decline. It made major changes to BLMC's board and management. Nevertheless, a better commercial decision would have been to break it up and leave the market to decide, but this would have been politically unacceptable.

The next few years saw the company make heroic efforts to attain commercial viability, but it was too small. More and more government funding was required, well above original estimates. Then came another change of direction. The government decided that it could no longer support BLMC and told the company to plan to 'privatise', recovered or not. This process involved the company management in activities that took them away from improving the company's performance.

At one stage the sale of Land Rover and the Truck operations to General Motors was agreed. It was, however, stopped at the very last minute by another government change of mind, and the company had to continue searching. The change of mind was entirely political, based on the fear that the sale to a foreign company might lose the government votes in sensitive constituencies. The extent to which this was misguided can be seen in subsequent history, when parts of BLMC have passed to American, German and Indian companies and additionally, in a small but significant way, to a Chinese company – all without the slightest protest. Indeed, these moves have been welcomed by the public.

By this time, just before the mid 1980s, privatisation work, which had been set at nought by government vacillation, had involved so much management effort that the company told the government that the pressure to privatise had to stop. This the government accepted – but only for a time.

In 1986, a new chief executive (Graham Day) took over with a clear remit to privatise. He succeeded. The company was sold to British Aerospace and from then on commercial considerations dictated what would happen to the company.

Over-optimism in Assessment of Prospects and in Forecasts

Hindsight has shown that there was consistent over-optimism from the management throughout the forty years covered in this book. This over-optimism applied to two main categories of forecasts.

The first category is made up of assessments of the company's broad prospects, such as the one made when it was decided to form BLMC; the one made by the Ryder team when government ownership was recommended; the decisions by British Aerospace and then BMW to buy the company; and finally the decision by the Phoenix consortium to run the remains of the original company as an independent entity.

The second category is made up of what may be called operational forecasts made within the company – mainly forecasts of vehicle sales both of current models and those from programmes of investment in new models. This over-optimism existed in very nearly all sales forecasts made throughout the life of the company.

Decision to Form BLMC

The assessment of the prospects of BLMC on which the decision to go ahead with its formation was made is examined at length in Chapter 2. At the time of formation there were enough signs of weakness, especially in the car companies that formed the major part of the whole. These weaknesses were not taken sufficiently into account, in the face of commercial pressures from the companies and a government belief that a large entity was necessary for commercial success. The result was that the prospects were undoubtedly on the optimistic, if perhaps not clearly over-optimistic, side of reality.

Whether a more realistic assessment of the difficulty of the task would have led to performance good enough to avoid the 1975 failure is doubtful. The management worked hard – lack of effort was not the cause of failure. The prime causes of failure are laid out in Chapter 12. A more realistic assessment of the difficulties facing the new company might have led to a stronger management being appointed, in which case a better outcome might have been achieved. But it is uncertain whether a stronger management team could have been found.

A further question is whether the management, once the company came into operation, recognised the problems fully or quickly enough. Broadly, the answer is 'No'. The over-optimism persisted, particularly the belief inherent in the original decision to form BLMC that large financial benefits would come from car product rationalisation. In theory, resources could be saved and concentrated on fewer models, thereby ensuring that each model would be more successful than its predecessor. In practice, rationalisation proved far more difficult to achieve than at first envisaged and, furthermore, new models were not successful.

All in all, the optimism of the original decision and its persistence played a significant role in the 1975 failure.

The Ryder Report

By the time the Ryder team made its recommendation that the government should, in effect, take ownership of BLMC, the weaknesses had been very clearly demonstrated. The team nevertheless ignored that reality and recommended carrying on with few significant changes except for an unrealistic recommendation to introduce a form of industrial democracy that was forecast to cure the industrial relations problems and bring considerable financial benefits. Inevitably, things carried on in the same way, the industrial democracy scheme failed to bring benefits and was allowed to lapse, and the board and much of the senior management had to be changed. If the original decision to form BLMC was at least over-optimistic to a degree, the Ryder recommendations were wildly over-optimistic and were the prime cause of the company failure continuing unchecked for a further two years.

Reviews by Purchasers of BLMC's Car Companies

British Aerospace was the first company to purchase the BLMC car and Land Rover businesses. There is no firm information of its assessment, but presumably commercial success was foreseen. However, that was overshadowed by the sale of those companies to BMW – a sale of immense benefit to British Aerospace. In the period of British Aerospace ownership, some efficiency improvements were achieved and that period can be assessed as one that slightly improved the commercial prospects of the purchased companies.

BMW was clearly over-optimistic in expecting a commercially successful outcome to the takeover of Rover Group. Among BMW senior management there was a high degree of doubt, but the enthusiasm of Bernd Pischetsrieder carried the day. He believed that the passion for the brands within Rover Group would be as powerful as the passion that was the basis of BMW's success, and that together the companies could turn this into exciting new products guaranteeing commercial success. Pischetsrieder was not fully aware of Rover's dependence on the collaboration with Honda. The belief that Rover Group management and engineers knew what success looked like and could deliver it lay behind the decision to leave them alone for far too long. In the end, the losses were too large for BMW to bear, and the consequence of their over-optimistic expectations was that the residual car business was left without the prospect of ever achieving commercial success.

The Last Burst of Over-optimism

The last burst of over-optimism came from the Phoenix consortium that purchased the remains of the BLMC car companies from BMW. The four, who included two BL senior executives, took on the task of establishing a viable company, essentially competing in the volume car market with two saloon car model lines plus a sports car with an initial total volume of less than 200,000 a year. Although initially well-financed, it was unrealistic to expect long-term success from such a start. Possibly another takeover or collaboration with a stronger company was hoped for. In the event the company failed – the last act of over-optimism.

Internal Over-optimistic Forecasts

A feature of the internal BLMC forecasts of car sales was the number of times those forecasts, whether used in plans, budgets or investment decisions, exceeded the actual sales by considerable margins. This was particularly true for the first seven-year period of decline. After that, the forecasts became more realistic but still continued to be over-optimistic to a significant extent,

How over-optimism affected the actual performance of the company is difficult to quantify. It is possible that seriously challenging budgeted sales forecasts could have led to extra efforts to raise the actual sales levels. However, business plans, manning levels and manufacturing facility plans were based on the sales forecasts. Under-performance led to surplus capacity and inefficient operation. More critically, difficult decisions over plant closure and redundancy were avoided. In the planning of new models, optimism resulted in unnecessary investment. A particular example was the high sales forecast used to set up the SD1 production facilities – dictated by BLMC management at a far higher level than the internal company forecast.

It is highly likely that the sequence of plans and budgets, each asking for a higher level of funding than the last one, increased the exasperation of its owner (the government) and was an important factor in the decision to privatise.

When BMW took over Rover, the fundamental difference in the companies' forecasting philosophy had an impact on how Rover was viewed by its new owners. Where Rover believed in 'stretch targets', BMW worked on the principle of 'under-forecast and over-deliver'. Throughout BMW, achievement of targets was the key performance measure for all individuals. Whatever circumstances change (e.g. exchange rate moves) individuals were expected to do everything to meet their original targets. Rover's constant failure to meet its targets contributed greatly to BMW's loss of confidence in the company.

Leadership

It is hard to say how much a single leader can influence the performance of a company. From the outset BLMC was an extremely complex organisation with a declining market share. Bringing about a fundamental change of direction was an extraordinarily difficult task. However, there were some outstanding examples of individual leaders who achieved this. Most notable was Michael Edwardes who saw labour relations and engineering deficiencies as his main challenges. He addressed both by taking on the unions and by starting the relationship with Honda. Similarly, John Egan realised when he took over as CEO of Jaguar that poor product quality was weakening the company. He mobilised the workforce to resolve problems. Sales and profitability improved dramatically and, as a result, Jaguar was able to be floated off.

The underlying problems of manufacturing and engineering were well known in the early days of BLMC. Each new product launch revealed serious failings. Field reports and quality surveys showed clearly the gap between the company's products and the competition. But the leaders did not have the single-minded drive to make product quality the overwhelming priority, nor did they fully appreciate the desperate need to bolster engineering resources and facilities. It was only in the 1990s that quality reached competitive (but not outstanding) levels.

Similarly, product rationalisation, which was the initial driving force behind the merger, was left unresolved for decades. It must be accepted that the separate brands required significant vehicle differentiation which militated against rationalisation. But this was not an argument to give up. Platform strategy, in which vehicle architecture and major components are shared between very different models and across different brands, is now common practice throughout the motor industry. This technique had not been developed in the 1970s, but commonising major components like engines was general practice. Forcing component sharing against the resistance of the separate companies required that the leaders understood the potential benefits and had the will to make it happen. This was sadly lacking

A recent example of how a leader can turn round a company that was losing market share and suffering massive losses is the recruitment from Boeing of Alan Mulally as CEO of Ford in September 2005. He immediately raised the funds to restructure the company by mortgaging its assets and selling off Aston Martin, Jaguar Land Rover and Volvo. Under his leadership product quality was given immediate priority, the Ford product range was rationalised and manufacturing sites were restructured, and the US workforce was reduced by 40 per cent. Ford managed to weather the financial crisis without government support, unlike GM and Chrysler. By 2010 Ford's market share had recovered and the company had returned to healthy profitability.

Substantial change can only occur with the cooperation of the workforce. In Germany and Japan the unions and the company work together to achieve sustainable growth in the highly competitive motor industry. Informed leadership is equally important for the unions. Long-term job security depends on the health of a company. Short-term sacrifices may be needed. By the 1990s, a much improved relationship between Rover and the unions had been achieved. However it was too late to save the company.

Jaguar Land Rover – Tata

The Jaguar XF, launched in 2008, was the new executive saloon replacing the S-type. (Jaguar Land Rover)

The Jaguar XJ, launched in 2009, was the sixth generation of the luxury saloon. (Jaguar Land Rover)

The Jaguar F-type, launched in 2012, was an all-new high performance sports car. (Jaguar Land Rover)

The Range Rover Evoque, launched in 2011, was a highly successful small luxury Range Rover, derived from the Freelander. (Jaguar Land Rover)

The fourth-generation Range Rover, launched in 2012, was an all-new aluminium-bodied premium 4x4. (Jaguar Land Rover)

The second-generation Range Rover Sport, launched in 2013, was a sports model derived from the new aluminium-bodied Range Rover. (Jaguar Land Rover)

Epilogue

At the time that BLMC was formed, the UK motor industry was producing just over 1.5 million cars per year. Very nearly half of these (47 per cent) were produced by BLMC. Since then BLMC has collapsed, Ford has withdrawn from UK vehicle manufacture and the Rootes Group no longer exists. Together these companies accounted for 87 per cent of UK production.

Today the UK still produces just over 1.5 million cars. It could be assumed that the Japanese transplants of Nissan, Toyota and Honda have filled the gap left by the British manufacturers. But this is not entirely the answer. The legacy of BLMC – Mini, Land Rover, Range Rover, Jaguar and even MG – still makes up 39 per cent of UK production.

The picture is not the same for commercial vehicles. In 1967 the UK produced 385,000 commercial vehicles; by 2013 this figure had fallen to 88,000. Two major manufacturers remain: Vauxhall, producing panel vans; and Leyland Trucks producing 6- to 18-ton trucks sold under the DAF brand. Leyland Trucks has its roots in BLMC and via a collaboration with DAF is now owned by a US truck manufacturer PACCAR inc.

The BLMC legacy brands may also not be British owned, but their success is helping the UK car industry achieve healthy growth in Europe's difficult trading conditions. It is worth recounting how this transformation has occurred.

Perhaps the greatest contribution has come from Land Rover. As we have seen in previous chapters, Ford purchased the company from BMW in 2000. From the outset, Ford was very careful to establish a fully functional organisation. The engineering team was set up by selecting some of the best Rover engineers and locating them at Gaydon, which had been established by BMW as the Rover Group test-and-development centre. Manufacturing was integrated at Solihull.

Much to the surprise of many, both within and outside the company, when its activities were separated from the overall Rover Group accounts, Land Rover was running at a substantial loss. Ford brought in Bob Dover, who had presided over the turnround of Aston Martin, as the senior executive. Bob Dover had previously worked at Land Rover and had a great feel for its heritage. Immediately he worked hard to instil a sense of pride and purpose in his new team. His task was to focus on the strength of the Land Rover and Range Rover brands, to implement a new product plan and to return the company to profitability.

At the time of the sale, BMW engineers had started working on a new Range Rover. Ford reached agreement with BMW to continue the project and the third-generation Range Rover was launched in 2002. The next project was the new Discovery. Several concepts had been worked on under BMW, but the Land Rover engineers started from scratch. This model was totally new and was launched in 2004. It broke new ground in terms of comfort and interior space without sacrificing any off-road capability.

After considerable internal debate, the (in some eyes) brave decision was taken to expand the Range Rover model range by adding a smaller, more sporting vehicle designed to compete with BMW's X5. This model, the Range Rover Sport, was derived from the new Discovery and was launched in 2005. Its importance cannot be underestimated. It exceeded sales expectations and played a major part in restoring Land Rover to profitability.

The next product in the Land Rover range to be addressed was the Freelander. A totally new model was engineered as part of a global Ford platform programme, which included the Mondeo replacement and the Volvo S80. The much improved Freelander 2 was launched in 2006. The final product, the Defender, remained an enigma. The Defender occupied a unique niche and despite much concept work neither BMW nor Ford could devise a financially acceptable way of replacing it. Instead the decision was taken to upgrade the model by installing a Ford engine, thus bringing to an end Land Rover's manufacture of engines. Ford management's renewal of Land Rover's product range was therefore complete.

While product direction was being settled, Ford set about modernising the Solihull production site. Through the years Solihull had grown like Topsy, although some of the facilities dated back to the Second World War. After substantial investment a much improved process flow was achieved as the new models were introduced.

Ford's purchase of Land Rover brought Jaguar and Land Rover together under the same ownership for the first time in sixteen years. Initially Ford kept the two organisations separate while Land Rover found its feet and future direction was established. After two years the organisations were integrated. At the time, Land Rover's fortunes were recovering but Jaguar's fortunes were waning. Recent new models, the S-Type and the X-Type, which were intended to exploit Jaguar's heritage, had failed to meet their sales targets. Work was under way on a new mid-engined sports car.

After the integration, Jaguar's priorities changed. The sports car project was dropped in favour of a replacement for the S-Type saloon, the contemporary XF, which was to be launched in 2007. The future of the X-Type was in doubt and no replacement was planned. The X-Type was manufactured at Halewood in Liverpool and it was decided to move Freelander production from Solihull to Halewood at the introduction of Freelander 2 to exploit Halewood's surplus capacity.

By 2007 Ford had therefore put in place the foundations of Jaguar Land Rover. A product plan was in place. Manufacturing efficiency and quality had improved substantially. Land Rover had returned to profitability and there was optimism that Jaguar would return to profitability with its new models. But all was not well at Ford. The US market was proving difficult as Japanese competition was eating into Ford's market share. Ford made the decision to retrench its activities and concentrate on the core Ford brands. Aston Martin, Jaguar Land Rover (JLR) and Volvo were all to be sold off. In the middle of 2007 a competition for the acquisition of JLR was started. Interest was high and there were several bidders who appreciated the value of the brands and the transformation that Ford had brought about.

By the start of 2008 the Indian conglomerate Tata had won the competition for JLR. Tata's intentions were clear from the outset. JLR would continue on the path laid out by Ford. The company would be treated as a wholly self-sufficient entity, the organisation would remain intact and resources would not be used to support Tata's automotive activities in India. The senior management under the leadership of David Smith would remain in place. The Jaguar XF was launched as planned at the end of 2007 during the transition from Ford to Tata. Work continued on the new Jaguar XJ saloon, which was due for launch in 2009.

And then came the global financial meltdown. Sales of all premium products throughout the world reduced dramatically. JLR found itself in a cash crisis. Discussions took place on the possibility of government support and even the closure of one of the Birmingham manufacturing plants (Land Rover's Solihull or Jaguar's Castle Bromwich). JLR managed to survive and recovered largely by making inroads into the markets less affected by the downturn – China, Russia and Saudi Arabia. Critically, new model development continued despite the difficult trading conditions.

As JLR recovered, a new management team was put in place under Ralf Speth who was an ex-BMW executive with direct experience of working at Land Rover. Speth recruited a number of ex-BMW personnel to strengthen the management team.

Perhaps the most important decision taken at this time was to work on a smaller Range Rover. As with the Range Rover Sport there was considerable debate within the company on whether a smaller, cheaper model would dilute the value of the Range Rover brand. The project was driven through and the Range Rover Evoque was launched to great acclaim in 2011. The Evoque's success was unprecedented and it now accounts for about a third of Land Rover volumes. It is the UK's highest-selling 4x4 and is the basis of JLR's growth in China.

Following the Evoque, the fourth-generation Range Rover and the second-generation Range Rover Sport were introduced in 2012 and 2013 respectively. These models share a completely new all-aluminium platform, which had started concept development before the Tata acquisition. As with all previous new Range Rover models, sales have exceeded expectations and Land Rover's growth continues unabated.

At Jaguar, following on from the XJ saloon, two new projects were started: the XF Sportsbrake, launched in 2012, and the new high-performance sports car, the F-Type, which followed in 2013. However, in 2013 Jaguar volumes were less than 20 per cent of total JLR volumes. The next phase of Jaguar's growth is the introduction of a new aluminium platform, which provides the technology for a range of vehicles including a full competitor for the BMW 3 Series.

Since 2008 JLR has been purchasing all of its engines from Ford and Peugeot. It has the capability to design engines but did not have engine-manufacturing facilities. This situation changed in 2014 when the new engine plant located in Wolverhampton started to produce an all-new JLR-designed engine.

In parallel with the growth at JLR, BMW's Mini has seen steady growth in volumes since its introduction in 2001. BMW had been working on the new Mini at the time of the sale of the Rover Group and decided to retain the brand and its UK manufacture. The Mini is manufactured at Cowley, Oxford, with the body panels sourced from Swindon, originally part of the Pressed Steel Fisher company. The first-generation new Mini had an engine that was designed by Chrysler and manufactured in Brazil. The transmission was produced on part of the Longbridge site that BMW retained.

Original sales forecasts for the new Mini were pessimistic at less than 100,000 per year. Actual sales far exceeded this and are now over twice the original estimate. The Mini is now in its third generation and although similar in appearance to the first generation it has been completely re-engineered. The engines are sourced from BMW's UK engine plant at Hams Hall and transmissions purchased from Getrag in Germany. The Longbridge transmission plant at Cofton Hackett closed in 2006.

The Mini product range has expanded with the introduction of larger versions exploiting the Mini style. These models are produced by Steyr in Austria. The design and engineering of the Mini range is entirely carried out by BMW in Munich. Front-wheel drive, once anathema to BMW, is now the basis of a platform that is shared with smaller BMW models. BMW's UK personnel are responsible for developing the UK models for volume production. Under BMW stewardship, considerable investment has been made at the Cowley plant to create an efficient process flow producing high-quality vehicles.

After JLR and the Mini at Cowley, BL's remaining link to the UK motor industry is at Longbridge. During the final months of its existence, MG Rover was in discussion with two Chinese manufacturers, Nanjing and SAIC (formerly the Shanghai Automotive Industry Corporation). Before its final collapse, MG Rover sold the design rights of the Rover 25 and 75 models to SAIC. MG Rover was also in discussion on the possibility of SAIC taking a controlling interest in the company. These talks came to nothing, and in April 2005 MG Rover went into receivership. After the collapse, Nanjing purchased the assets, which included the rights to the MG brand, and then shipped plant and equipment to China. At this time Nanjing retained leases on part of the Longbridge site and announced plans to recommence vehicle production. It was not until after Nanjing had merged with SAIC that limited build of the MGF sports car restarted in 2008.

Once SAIC had taken control of Nanjing's interests it put in place more ambitious plans for Longbridge. SAIC is the largest of the Chinese motor companies, producing nearly 4 million cars per year. Its product designs are licensed from VW and General Motors. The licences largely limit sales to within China. SAIC needed to develop the capability to create its own products. This would open up world markets for SAIC products.

The Longbridge site provided the opportunity to build a research-and-development centre manned by experienced motor industry engineers.

SAIC enthusiastically set about the task of creating its R&D centre. Within a year more than 400 people had been recruited. The bulk of the engineers were previously employed at MG Rover. The role of the R&D centre is twofold: first, to design new products; and second, to train the growing team of SAIC's highly qualified but inexperienced engineers in the process of new model creation. The MG brand has become the brand for SAIC's 100 per cent owned products in all world markets. The first MG Roewe 550 based on the Rover 75 was launched in China in 2008 and the all-new MG 6 was launched in 2010. The MG 6 is manufactured in China and assembled at Longbridge from Chinese components. The MG 6 was followed by the smaller MG 3 in 2013.

After the Second World War, Major Ivan Hirst was instrumental in bringing VW back into production and in 1975 George Turnbull (later Sir George Turnbull) led the team that set up Hyundai's first factory in South Korea. It is interesting to speculate whether SAIC's R&D centre at Longbridge will play a similar role in the future of the Chinese motor industry. Only time will tell.

The resurgence of the UK's car industry is not limited to BLMC's legacy brands. The UK is a major producer of engines, making over a million more engines than vehicles. The UK-based luxury brands – Rolls-Royce, Bentley and Aston Martin – are all thriving. The UK is the largest and most successful centre for the world's motor sport industry. Nissan and Ford have large design and engineering centres in the UK. All of this activity is dependent on schools and universities training an increasing number of skilled engineers motivated to enter the motor industry and create the technology that is essential for long-term survival. It is daunting to know that Chinese universities are producing over a million graduate engineers every year.

Author Profiles

Mike Carver (1922–2015)

Mike left school in 1940 as soon as he was 18, to join the RAF. In 1963, having reached the rank of Group Captain and been awarded the Air Force Cross for his flying activities, he decided to retire early and try other fields of work. He joined the Ford Motor Company as a financial analyst, but quickly became a manager, working on financial matters related to investments, product costs and profitability. In 1968 he joined BLMC as a manager in the newly-formed central finance staff, with responsibilities for investment and product profitability. After about two years, his role was changed to responsibility for product policy coordination and when Rover-Triumph was formed he became director of product planning and a member of that company board. When BLMC failed in 1975 he was seconded to the NEB as head of the staff responsible for the NEB's monitoring and control of the company. When the BLMC's failure continued he was involved in the decision to change the board and some management. Subsequently, Michael Edwardes, the new chairman and chief executive, took him back into the company as director of corporate planning. After some years in this role he became group executive director and a member of the main board. Following his retirement from the company in 1989 he held various part-time posts, the main ones being adviser to Honda on European affairs and a non-executive director of Unipart. He was also awarded the OBE. Mike passed away in June 2015, having fulfilled his ambition to have the story of British Leyland told 'from the inside'.

Anne Youngson (b.1947)

Anne read English at Birmingham University and started work in the sales forecasting department at Longbridge in 1970. She moved to Pirelli Tyres as marketing services manager for three years but returned in 1976 and held various staff positions working on the Honda relationship and within product planning and strategic planning. She moved into project management within the product development division and ran concept development projects in Land Rover and a new vehicle launch team within Rover Cars. She was the only woman at this level in product development. Her final position was as head of the special vehicles operation in Land Rover, designing, engineering, manufacturing and selling derivatives for specialist customers. Having taken early retirement in 2003, she has created a second career as a consultant on skills development, and has completed an MA in creative writing.

Nick Seale (b. 1945)

Nick read mechanical engineering at Birmingham University and joined Ford as a graduate engineer in 1967. After spending time in engine design he moved to finance as a senior financial analyst. In 1973 he joined BLMC as part of Mike Carver's product policy co-ordination team. After Ryder, Nick took a role as a component product planning manager. Under Michael Edwardes, Nick was responsible for business planning in the newly formed Austin-Morris company. From there he joined the Honda negotiating team. His next assignment was responsibility for the product planning of Rover Group's advanced vehicles. In the final phase of his career at Rover, Nick returned to engineering, eventually heading up the Rover power train engineering function under BMW. At Land Rover he was responsible for the concept engineering of future products. Nick retired in 2003 and since then has curated an exhibition on green technologies, been a Sherpa for an EU Commission report on the motor industry (CARS 21) and latterly become a Principal Fellow of Warwick University.

Index